PARENT POWER

NAVIGATE SCHOOL AND BEYOND

PUNAM V. SAXENA, M.ED.

LEADING POINTS PUBLISHING

PARENT POWER

Navigate School and Beyond

Punam V. Saxena, M.Ed.

Library of Congress Control Number: 2021903257

First edition May 2021

Cover design by Aparna Verma of Design Reach
www.aparnaverma.com

ISBN 978-1-7366402-0-3 (hardback)
ISBN 978-1-7366402-1-0 (paperback)
ISBN 978-1-7366402-2-7 (ebook)

www.punamvsaxena.com

To my extended family who has loved and supported me unconditionally.

To my parents who have guided me throughout my life.

To my bachchas Maya, Kavi, Lyla, and India who have given me purpose and pride.

To Anu who has given me the confidence to share my voice.

CONTENTS

PRAISE FOR PARENT POWER

"A fantastic book! I especially LOVE Punam's perspectives. She's inspiring and motivating, yet real and honest. Highly recommend this book!"

-Allison Dillard, Author of *Crush Math Now and Raise Your Math Grade*

"There's a lot of good concrete parenting suggestions in this book. But, if I had to choose the one piece of advice, it would be to carve out time for yourself, take care of yourself. Punam's parenting has produced happy and successful children. That happened mostly because she understood the value in being happy herself."

-Nicole Phillips, Elementary School Educator

"Punam offers a refreshingly honest view on how to navigate the education system to benefit your kids -- and stay sane in the process. Her perspectives provide tips to help you, all while admitting she hasn't always followed her own advice. Every parent should read this!" -Lenore Devore, Former Editor of *The Ledger*

"Here's what I know about Punam Saxena, she will never stop being an advocate for parents and their children especially when it comes to the education system. She is the bridge that all parents seek when faced with challenges, uncertainty, and doubt. *Parent Power* is a map of how to maneuver through the education system with ease all while taking care of yourself and your child. Punam weaves together personal stories, inspiration, and immediately useful actions. If you've been looking for some direction to ensure your child has the most rewarding educational experience, *Parent Power* is the compass."

    -Kathy Barron, author of *Token of Choice*

"Authentic, insightful, and compassionate guide for all stages of parenting. You will find inspiration in these pages. Through beautifully woven stories of personal experience with intuitive wisdom, it naturally provokes thoughtful reflection and inspired action. It will be of great benefit to all who read it."

    -Dr. Reshma M. Patel, Functional Medical Physician

"It is WONDERFUL! So many helpful tools and I love the Punam's Perspective parts the best. Being real and honest is such a gift to other parents."

    -Sara Roberts McCarley, Randy Roberts Foundation

"In *Parent Power,* Punam Saxena draws on her decades of experience as a parent and educator to clearly, gently, and without judgement guide parents through the "long game" of being a partner in educating their children. Providing both practical tools and big picture ideas, Saxena moves past the anxiety-producing social structures of modern parenting and encourages parents to draw on their own strength and their community and familial resources to guide their children, collaborate with teachers, and actually *enjoy* the process of parenting children through their school years and beyond. Particularly in the midst of a pandemic, Saxena's advice on self-care and moving beyond parenting guilt provide a balm for over-stretched parents, but, the lessons of *Parent Power* extend well beyond these difficult times and it is a must-read for any parent!"

-Dr. Natalie Boero, Professor of Sociology,
San Jose State University and parent of twin teenagers

FOREWORD

INTRODUCTION

Teachers are servant leaders in many ways. They help impart the knowledge and social skills needed for children to succeed, expecting only in return that their students perform their best. Teachers are also true heroes as they work diligently to ensure every student remains inquisitive about learning. By inspiring students to attain a deeper understanding of topics, teachers can create lifelong learners. But they cannot do it alone. They need cooperation from parents and the community as volunteers in the classroom, as supporters for the school, and as advocates at the state and district levels.

So, who exactly are teachers? Are they only the formal ones that you have had in the classroom? Probably not.

Reflect on the people you've met throughout your life.

Most likely, you have interacted with thousands of people through work, family, and social gatherings. Each one of them has taught you something. It may have been a concept, a life-lesson, or something minuscule, but every single person has taught you something.

Growing up as a person of Indian heritage in a rural town

in Georgia in the 1970s, there was a lot to learn. We were the only Indians in the city for the first 12 years we lived there. In fact, in those days, we were frequently asked which tribe we belonged to as many did not even know India was a separate country. They just assumed that being Indian meant someone indigenous to the United States and therefore was affiliated with a tribe.

We were such an anomaly that the local newspaper interviewed us and put us on the front page, where we shared parts of our culture with the community. Yes, there was a lot of learning taking place back then. We needed to assimilate to this new culture and understand the nuances of American life in order to embrace our new home. Over the years, I managed to find a niche in our community in which I rarely shared any controversial opinions with anyone or offered challenging viewpoints without being asked. I was coasting and biding my time until I could find a group of like-minded individuals.

When I went off to college in the big city of Atlanta, it was exciting to think there would be a peer group with similar backgrounds who faced the same cultural challenges that I had. I was looking forward to interacting and commiserating with people who looked, talked, and thought like me. And though, I met some fantastic friends whom I respect and love even to this day, I was still searching for my place in the world—still looking for my passion and my peeps.

A year after graduation, I married and moved to hot, sunny Florida, where I began adjusting to the new life that my husband—an engineer also of Indian descent—and I were building together. And yet, I was still searching.

B.C. (Before Children), I was a special education teacher specializing in teaching students with severe emotional and learning disabilities, and those on the autism spectrum. Each day, I was reminded to applaud my students' small accomplishments. Their successes meant that I, as a teacher, had accomplished something, too. It occurred to me that building self-confidence in these students, being present in their lives, and providing support was crucial to their academic, social, and emotional well-being. I was beginning to feel the source of my passion and desire stirring.

A few years later, I became a mother to four beautiful children in the span of five years. For those wondering, my last two were twins and like most parents, I struggled to balance parenting and finding my purpose in life—my passion. I was overwhelmed, exhausted, and many times, I was in over my head.

A.C. (After Children), my husband and I decided that I would stay home and become the Lead Parent. My job of caring for them led to volunteering at the school, district, and state levels advocating for all students. With four children, I was keeping myself busy with their activities, but I was still yearning for something more, something that fulfilled my internal desire to share my talents with the world. Fast forward 20+ years. My children are all in their twenties now and I can be more reflective and critical about my child-rearing skills.

How did I parent? What did I learn? Can my experience help others?

Often, when my children were in school, I was asked by other parents about my ability to create relationships and trust with my children's teachers and administrators. I usually chuckled (to myself), wondering if it was a serious question because it seemed logical to me. I came to realize that they really were curious. My friends truly wanted to know how I managed to become a partner in the educational process. This forced me to step back and assess how this journey began and how it transformed this SAHM (Stay at Home Mom) into someone who becomes passionate about enhancing the educational experience of students, working with the school, and enjoying a bond of trust and friendship with the faculty and staff.

So, let me share this journey with you.

When my children started school, I would volunteer as a way to connect with the school, and, quite frankly, to feel connected to something outside the confines of the home. It started in the media center: shelving books, checking them in and out, and doing general media center volunteer duties. But I also volunteered for every classroom activity I could because I wanted to see my children in their school "environment." Volunteering allowed me to see how they interacted with their teachers and classmates, but it also allowed me to use my education degree in a non-bureaucratic way and work *with* the teacher. In essence, I was spying on my offspring—what every good parent does!

Soon, I found myself in leadership positions of parent organizations. The principals, faculty, and staff were becoming my friends and I was enjoying it immensely. I was finally engaged in a purpose, and yes, dare I say it, even becoming passionate about it.

Over the course of their educational careers, my children attended five schools. With each school, I found more passion, more engagement, and more responsibility. When they were in middle and high school, I was not only a volunteer, but I also became a confidante of the teachers and administrators. They felt I could walk both sides of the aisle—being an educator and a parent—and providing feasible solutions to issues related to the school and the parent organizations.

I became the president of the parent organizations in middle and high school, where I often fielded questions from other parents and ensured that students received what they needed without compromising the faculty, staff, and administrators' needs. I was offered these roles because of the relationship and trust I built with the schools—and especially with the adults in those schools.

How does one do that? I did it organically by being genuine and solution-oriented. And the most important attribute I had was being open to learning new things.

Now granted, I had the time as a "stay in the car mom" (I was NEVER home!) to build these relationships as I felt it was my job to be involved in their schools. I also recognize that not every parent has the ability or capability to do so. In this book, we will discuss how ALL of us can make an impact on our children's education, whether you are a "stay in the car" parent like I was, a career parent, or something in between.

I come from a family of educators. Whether they are teachers by profession or not, they inherently taught me something. This is the beauty of education. Learning something from everyone we meet and creating our own path in life.

Indulge me for a just a moment as I share what some important people in my life have taught me.

My oldest was our guinea pig, as is generally the case with the firstborn. We wanted to be the model parents. However, we gave up on that pipe dream somewhere between the extreme exhaustion and sleep deprivation. Yet, she persevered and succeeded despite us. She is one of the smartest and compassionate people I know.

And then . . .

Two years later, our son came along and rocked our world. We barely had a handle on raising one child, how were we going to manage two? He was a typical boy—curious and active, who kept us on our toes (and still does). He is our family cheerleader, always there to pick us up when we falter.

But wait! There's more!

Two and a half years later came our twins, a girl and a boy

born two minutes apart. We doubled our parent-child ratio in one fell swoop. Now, we were really in for a ride. Talk about being sleep-deprived . . . we had no idea!

Our older twin was and still is very particular in her approach to everything. She would observe, research, and then act. In fact, even today if our family wants something vetted thoroughly, we ask her to help. She is very thoughtful, kind, and an incredibly organized young lady. Our younger twin is a thinker and more laid back. He is so laid back that I have to remind him to get riled up sometimes. His approach to life is, "Everything happens for a reason, so let it play out." He is definitely the calm in the Saxena storm.

My children are the precious gems in my life. And while I enjoyed all of the time spent raising them, I still was looking for my passion. And while I tried to and get a handle on what that might be, I looked to my role models for lessons:

- From my mother, who taught second grade, I learned what patience could look like. I am still learning to be more patient as I grow older, but at least I know what it looks like.
- From my dad, who was a professor, I learned resilience. He persevered after he immigrated to America, raised us, and then sent us on our way to be independent.
- From my brother, a doctor, I have learned to be more open-minded and reflective in my actions. That my way is not always the *best* way—or even the only way.
- From my husband, I learned the hard lesson of not getting worked up over the small things. I continue to work on focusing on the important parts of life every single day.

- From my children who are on their way to being independent professionals of their own, I learned to love unconditionally. Each day they remind me by their words and actions that love is what carries us through life.

Parent Power is written to help parents realize that they are not alone. Parenting is a long game, and with knowledge and the help of a supportive team, we can all ensure our children are on the path to success and we can enjoy the journey in the process.

So, let's go!

ONE

TAKE CARE OF YOURSELF

How on earth can I find time for myself? I am knee-deep in trying to finish cooking, washing and putting up laundry, and then getting the kids ready for bed. Deadlines are looming at work and I'm exhausted. There's no time for me to even *think* about myself, much less take care of myself.

Does this sound like you? Between work, housework, children, and family, we are overcommitted and overextended, and it can be impossible to imagine finding any time for ourselves.

We have all seen those commercials that depict a perfect life: the house is spotless, and everyone is smiling and looks happy. And we think to ourselves, "How is this possible?" Then there are other commercials where the mess is strewn throughout the house, children are hanging on their parents, and everyone looks unkempt. These "commercial" parents are hanging on by a thread. They look tired and mentally exhausted. And in that case, we think, "Surely they can do better. They could use some self-care." When we take a moment to reflect and look at our own lives, we realize we are probably somewhere in between these two extremes.

According to Ricelle Concepcion, clinical psychologist and president of the Asian American Psychological Association, "Not only does self-care have positive outcomes for you, but it also sets an example to younger generations as something to establish and maintain for your entire life."

As parents, we do not generally prioritize our own mental and physical needs in the mayhem of our daily obligations. However, ironically, taking care of ourselves can help decrease the frequency of those days of mayhem, or at the very least, make them less overwhelming. We must develop strategies to help ourselves stay calm and remain productive.

Parent Time-Out

What is Parent Time-Out? When you become frustrated by your child's behavior, or, quite frankly, anyone else's, it's hard not to become irritated and possibly blow your stack. The instinct is to put your child in time-out. Time-outs are designed to diffuse a potentially volatile situation and give the parent and child some time to cool off by removing them from each other's physical space. Children go to their rooms or a corner of the room to spend a few minutes thinking about their actions and how they should modify their behavior. Many of us do this to reprimand our children. And like all rewards or punishments, it can work sometimes and not others.

What if you reversed roles? What if you, as a parent, put yourself in time-out? Let your children know that their behavior is frustrating you and you need some time alone to calm down. It may seem like an odd approach, but it can be quite powerful and effective. By putting yourself in time-out, children will usually stop and wonder what YOU did. When they ask, your response is simple. "I need a few minutes to think about how to make this situation better. I am becoming frustrated because I asked you to do something, and you are not doing it. So, before I lose my cool, I'm going to think about how I can better explain my request."

This behavior will usually stop them in their tracks because they are puzzled, thinking, "What did I do to illicit this reaction from you?" It also allows them to think about their behavior and how to "do better" next time. The bonus? The task you have asked them to do multiple times, which frustrated you in the first place, is likely to be completed because they want to make you happy. Children do not like it when their parents are upset and will usually try to make you happy which ensures their happiness, too.

This technique should only be used when you are sure it will have the most impact and be most effective. Used routinely, children become accustomed to it, and the technique becomes less impactful. Quite frankly, this goes for all behavior-modification techniques.

Now I know many of you are wondering why this is considered a part of parent self-care. Well, for a moment, think about the alternative. What happens if you do not diffuse the situation and put your child or yourself in time-out? The problem could likely escalate into one or both of you having a meltdown. Logically, we want to diffuse the situation and keep our blood pressure in check.

Taking care of ourselves is **self-care**. Knowing your limits, not crossing them, and putting yourself in a healthy situation for you and your children, **_Bam!_** Self-care!

Breathe!

According to Erin Leyba, Ph.D, "Doing a short breathing or meditation exercise can bring focus back to what is grounding and important." Yoga and meditation are beneficial to both mental and physical well-being.

In yoga, finding your breath is crucial to finding your body's center and staying grounded. Although it looks easy when you "strike the pose," you may not be getting the full benefits of yoga. To get those benefits, you must perform each pose properly, with the correct breathwork and focus. For most of us, this is tough, especially when you are operating at 100 mph. But accepting this challenge and stopping to focus on your breathing will bring you closer to positive results. Breathing, yoga, and meditation are all activities we can do to help us find calm in our crazy lives. These activities help release toxins so our bodies become healthier and more productive.

If you are looking for a mantra to help you relax, try something simple: "Breathe." Close your eyes, take a deep breath in, and slowly release it. Repeat. It sounds benign and even overly simplistic, and yet it is challenging to implement. Often, if you are in the middle of an activity, it is hard to take a break to practice breathing. However, if the activity is causing anxiety, frustration, or anger, it is best to step back and take a breath. Focusing on your breath will allow you to relax, find calm, and re-center yourself before you begin again.

Happy Hour (HH)

Most of us think of Happy Hours (HH) as going out and having drinks with our friends. But not all Happy Hours require you to go out or to have an adult beverage. So, what does a HH actually entail then?

It means gathering with our friends, in person or virtually, to spend time, connect, and create memories. A HH also means that we are, by default, decompressing and relaxing by laughing and getting our minds off our daily stressors. It is essential to shift our focus away from our children and families every once in a while. We need to learn (or re-learn) that a healthy self is vital to our well-being. We should not feel guilty about it—more on that later.

HH is a wonderful way to connect with your peers, share your thoughts (child-related or not), and enjoy being an adult for a while. It also reminds you that you are a fun person and not the bore your child may sometimes think you are.

We need these opportunities to reconnect with the outside world and reset our bearings. It is imperative for our physical and mental well-being. HHs are not always conveniently timed, though. When you have children at home, you must schedule time for socializing. If not, all your time can easily be filled with homework, cooking meals, or other routine-but-necessary activities. Carving out time for yourself is exciting and important, especially when your friends are waiting for you.

Book Clubs/Reading/Journaling

We hear a lot about reading, book clubs, and journaling these days. They help to immerse ourselves in another's story and bring to light our own imaginations. Books take you to places you may never visit or even be able to imagine without the author's depictions. They expand your mind and knowledge.

Finding time to read may seem daunting to a busy, over-worked parent. How can I find 30 minutes to read for pleasure in my day? "Come on," is likely what you are thinking. And rightly so. Reading during naptime or before bed may be one option for you. It seems easier to accomplish a task when we create a routine and prioritize it. Although reading and other activities may need to fall off your radar for a while when your children are very young, it is necessary to understand that this is indeed a passing phase, and that they won't be little forever! It's hard to imagine, but this is a season in your life and, as seasons naturally do, they pass into another one.

I will confess, I was a voracious reader B.C. (before children). A.C. (after children), not so much. I couldn't find the time. As my children got older, when they could complete their homework independently and not need as much hands-on attention, I found time to sit down and read for my own enjoyment. My love for books has returned now that my children are older, and I am even able to create annual goals for how many books to read. This keeps me accountable. Finding what works for you and creating an attainable goal will make your self-care activities more tangible and successful—and reading really is an important self-care activity!

Book clubs force you to stay on a schedule. Most of us do well with a plan, and if we're held accountable by our friends, we are more likely to find the time to read. One of the great things about book clubs is that they keep you motivated to read a book at a certain pace and at the end, you get a great reward in the form of a HH with your friends. If you don't know of a book club to join, create one. Find a few friends who you enjoy hanging out with and start your own book club.

What about journaling? Journaling can also be an integral part of our self-care routine, as well. It's a great way to spend a few minutes alone with your thoughts. Many therapists ask their clients to journal without judgement or fear to detect behavior patterns, find opportunities to diffuse any negative or diminishing thoughts, and reflect on their innermost thoughts and feelings to prescribe constructive actions.

Often when putting pen to paper (or fingers to keyboard), we can find our calm and peace because it comes from honesty and reflection, which is therapeutic and healing.

Exercise

So many of us have a love/hate relationship with exercise. Every New Year, we all resolve to exercise more, eat healthier, and be committed to a new lifestyle. Then by the time February rolls around, most of us have already fallen off the wagon.

We envy our friends exercising, feeling energetic, and accomplishing feats we wish we could. We want to be healthy and to feel good, but the thought of all those hours of exercising can be mind-boggling. Once again, how do we find the time?

Exercise does not always mean going to the gym. Get the stroller out and push your child during a brisk walk. Go up and down the stairs 20 times. Buy some inexpensive exercise bands, balls, or dumbbells and watch some YouTube videos to learn some moves.

According to an article on betterhealth.vic.gov, even 30 minutes a day can be beneficial. It can:

- Provide mental breaks
- Increase blood flow and endorphins
- Increase energy level
- Allow you to do something good for yourself
- Burn calories
- Help you lose weight if that is one of your goals
- Increase positive moods

Who wouldn't want these benefits? So, find a physical activity that can help you keep moving, that you enjoy, and to which you are willing to commit. And if you just cannot find the time for "official" exercise, then vacuum more vigorously. Take the heavy garbage bags out—play frisbee with the kids.

Walk the dog. Turn your daily activities into your exercise routine.

Dance Party

Along the same lines of exercising, a dance party can be tons of fun and have the same benefits of exercising that we discussed above. A dance party is a time to listen to your favorite music, create an open area in your house, and enjoy dancing with your favorite people. Dancing to your favorite tunes can be nostalgic, taking you back to a time when you were young. Having a dance party with your family, is an excellent chance for you to create those unforgettable memories with your child.

In the town where I grew up, we would skate every Friday night at the local roller-skating rink. There were some great tunes and even better memories from those days. My children love hearing those stories of how music impacted my life, and they are amused by the fact that I was ever coordinated enough to roller skate.

A dance party offers the benefits of exercise while also enjoying the beat of the music.

Start the Day Early or Stay Up Late

We all need some quiet time for reflection. Finding time to be by ourselves and plan our days can be difficult during the bulk of the day. When our children are up, or we are at work, and often running frantically from one task to another, time can be limited for 'just thinking.'

If you are a morning person, you can start your day early. Waking up even a half-hour before everyone else wakes up can help you find your Zen for the day. You can start the day peacefully and on your terms. Then the day is yours to conquer.

This may reduce the frequency of the days that begin hurriedly when you are rushing through the morning routine. Starting behind the 8-ball can be both frustrating and unproductive.

But not all of us are morning people. If you are a night owl, evenings are your time to relax and unwind. Staying up late, spending time watching your favorite show, reading a book, or meditating can allow you to relax after a long day and plan for the next. This is also an integral piece of your self-care. If you can go to bed with a restful mind, you will sleep better and wake up more refreshed the next morning.

Grace

Grace is something that is difficult to exhibit for parents who are under stress. There exists an unrealistic image of what a perfect parent should be. We look around and see all of these adults who seemingly have the ideal life with the perfect children, the Better-Homes-and-Gardens house, and the perfect relationship with their spouse. And because we compare ourselves to them, finding grace for our "imperfect" lives can be difficult.

Perfection is an unreasonable expectation we have of ourselves and our children; no one has a perfect life. We all falter each day in some way. This is where grace comes in. Our vision of parenthood must include grace. We must give ourselves leeway when things do not go the way we would like and when we fall short of what we expect of ourselves. This includes times when we are too exhausted to prepare a meal and end up making frozen chicken tenders and fries, or when we are short on patience with our children through no fault of their own.

We beat ourselves up unnecessarily: Why did I lose my

patience over something so minor? Why didn't I make a healthier meal?

Our children, as they become older, really do not remember the times we fell short. Traumatic experiences aside, the moments they remember are the positive ones. They reflect on the quality time we spend with them instead of the quantity.

So, go ahead, allow yourself some grace, space to be human, to be fallible, and to be OK with it. Your mental health is more important than the perfect house, the perfect meal, and the ideal life. Giving yourself grace is likely the most powerful tool you can put in your arsenal for personal self-care. Use it often, use it for your sanity, and use it proudly.

Punam's Perspective

How do you carve out quiet time for your mental peace? It is an absolute must to know what works for you. How do you carve out quiet time for your mental peace? You are the best judge of your schedule, your abilities, and what will indeed be useful. Taking care of yourself is not selfish. It's necessary for your health and continued productivity, be it personal or professional. And when you take care of yourself, you can be a more calm, productive parent.

The ideas I have shared with you are all ones I have used while raising my children. I am here to tell you that I failed many times in implementing many of these methods. But the next day, I would pick myself up and try to do better than the day before. Parenting is the toughest and most important job there is. Some days will go perfectly, and all of the stars miraculously align, while on other days you won't be able to get through an hour without something going awry.

When my children were little, my self-care time was almost

nil. I never saw it as a priority and, consequently, there were some (who am I kidding? many) not-so-good days. Days when my patience was short, my exhaustion was high, and my output was less than stellar.

Now that my children are older, I realize that those younger years were the times I *needed* to take care of myself the most because my children needed me the most. When your children need you the most, you should be well-rested and relaxed in order to focus on everyone's needs.

As my children grew up and became more independent, I finally realized this and began to take better care of myself. It was the first time in my life I began to see how attending to my own needs made our home life better. I was calmer. I felt more empowered and mentally stronger. I could take better care of my family because I wasn't constantly struggling to find some "me" time since I had intentionally carved it out in my daily routine. In fact, making "me time" a planned for, consistent part of my routine actually made the process easier. I was already used to planning everything else, adding a slot for my self-care was simply doing what I already knew how to do: schedule my days.

I share this anecdote of my own life with you to illustrate the importance of self-care. Taking care of yourself is a necessary part of having a happy family. When we feel good about ourselves, we can accomplish much more. And become efficient in the process.

So, I encourage you to read your favorite book on the sofa, go for a walk, or whatever your preferred method of relaxation and self-care is. It may feel selfish at first, but by prioritizing your health, you create a home environment that is serene, tranquil, and purposeful.

TWO

GOT GUILT?

Parent guilt, that is. What is it? And why do we have it?

Parent guilt emerges from wishing we had done something related to or for our children that we did not. It could also mean something(s) we did with our children that we wish we did not do. We may feel guilty because of the many tasks we need or want to complete that may hinder our ability to have fun and relax with our family. Conversely, we may induce anxiety when we do take some time for ourselves because we feel deep down, we should always be busy tending to family or career matters. We have a work deadline to meet. Your child has a major school project to complete. There is a professional meeting. The family is hungry, or the house is a mess. These are just some of the challenges we face every day. They all demand our attention. They all deserve our attention, and yet we yearn for more uninterrupted and meaningful time with our children.

These are some of the sources of *Parent Guilt*.

And full disclosure here: I am riddled with it. I want more time with my children. Even now when they are independent and living their own lives.

Quality v. Quantity

While we all want more time with our children, is it time that we really want? Or do we want the times we *are* together to be more memorable and meaningful? This is the whole dialogue of quality v. quantity.

Brigid Schulte, a Pulitzer Prize-winning reporter for *The Washington Post*, quotes Melissa Milke, a sociologist at the University of Toronto and her co-authors as saying, "the more times teens spend with their parents together in family time, such as during meals, the less likely they are to abuse drugs and alcohol and engage in other risky or illegal behavior." Interesting, right? Quality of time seemingly does indeed matter. We often fail to realize that the quality of time we spend together can impact our children in the present and in the future.

I will share a story here that recently happened because it can't wait until the end of the chapter for Punam's Perspective.

My daughter and I were chatting about one of my edu-Nars (weekly webinars), where I was discussing my lack of patience with her and her siblings while they were growing up and how I felt that I had not created enough opportunities to spend time with them.

Her immediate response, without hesitation, was: "Mom, I don't remember those times. I remember all the great things you did for us and how much fun we had doing them."

Not often am I speechless, but I was speechless. It was at that moment I realized that the *quality* of our time together was actually more important than the *quantity* of time we spent together.

Having that quality time is vital because, if we are honest with ourselves, children are not counting the hours on the clock. They are counting the memories we make with them.

Our biggest challenge is to change *our* mindset on how we feel about our time with our children. We should allow ourselves to be OK with not having the quantity of time with our children IF we are creating memorable quality moments. If we are making the times that we are together exciting and fun, then we are doing a good job—even if it is 30 minutes a day that we have to spend with them before heading off to that meeting or finishing that work project. That counts. All quality time with your children counts.

Don't Compare

We all compare. We look at others and determine our self-worth depending on what we observe. We are often looking at people and believe they are living this Utopian life which we want to emulate.

Few of us are immune. We want what others have: their cars, outfits, or house. Or we are envious because they are civically engaged in every prominent committee you can imagine and always dressed to the nines. They have perfect children and a perfect spouse. They are exuding all of the qualities that society deems to be great. But what happens behind closed doors when no one is looking?

Their lives are just as crazy as the rest of us. They are running around trying to get everything done, just like we are. I guarantee you they are wearing their grungy clothes and certainly are not dressed to the nines 24/7, trying to make it all happen. They are having family issues, just like us. The problems may be different, but we all face challenges at some point while raising our children.

The secret is: Don't compare.

This is my husband's favorite line. By comparing, we are selling ourselves short of all the extraordinary qualities we hold and the incredible things we are doing in our own lives. We are diminishing our accomplishments to meet someone else's standard. In essence we let comparison steal the joy we've been given by falsely assuming that their joy is better.

Give yourself more credit—pat yourself on the back. Be proud of what you are doing and what you have accomplished. No one can take away what you have achieved. By comparing yourself to others, you lessen your self-worth and you will forever be chasing the whims of what someone else defines as worthwhile.

Get a Grip, People

You are overworked, overcommitted, and, many times, just plain over *it*. You are running around like a crazy person. Your inner voice is saying, "Get a grip! If it's not life or death, you need to take a deep breath." The idea here is to focus on what matters most—and the truth is that most things (at least the ones we worry about) do not matter that much.

As a gentle reminder, children may require a lot from us. But they *need* very little. They need food, clothes, shelter, and love. That is all they need. But somehow, we seem to think we need to sew matching outfits for our children (guilty), paint personalized cornhole boards with their university's logo (guilty), and create monogrammed travel pillows for their sleepover party favors (again, guilty).

Yes, clearly, someone needs to relax!

When we look at what we *need* to do and what we *are* doing, we should be grateful if we are able to do something special for and with our children. So, take a moment to enjoy the rewards of all you have accomplished. And if you aren't able to complete a task, give yourself some grace and realize that you are doing the best you can at that moment.

That is all we can do. That is all we should and can expect from ourselves.

Take a step back and assess what absolutely needs to be accomplished. Finding calm in the middle of a storm shows strength and resilience. Remember to focus on what's important.

When You Can't Relax Because You're the Host of the Party

You have the dubious honor of hosting the next social event. Now your *Parent Guilt* has likely just increased tenfold. The time you would normally spend with your children may decrease because of the desire to host the perfect event. So, why not ask the children to help? Here are some ways to help engage your children, teach them organizational skills, and have you feel less guilty in the process:

- If the event is not a potluck style, divide the tasks between your family members. Everyone older than 4 can take a task or two off your plate, even something as simple as setting the cutlery on the table. This will allow them to feel included in the event and proud of their participation.
- Praise them for their efforts. It will likely be different than the way you would do it but, again, prioritize what is essential and needs to be completed.

Your goal is to decrease your Parent Guilt and increase your time with your children. Find ways to carve out that time. And sometimes, that time can be working together for the greater good.

. . .

Note: The next two sections discuss topics that you should consult with your physician if you have questions. I am NOT a physician. Only your doctor can give you accurate health advice for you and your family.

Screen Time v. Real-Time

Unfortunately, we are all guilty of using devices to keep our children occupied. Mayo Clinic has shared guidelines on how much time children should spend looking at a screen during their early years. Now, I am forewarning you, you're not going to like these numbers.

These are the recommended screen time guidelines for children:

- Birth-18 months: Only video chatting. No games, no TV, no iPad.
- 18-24 months: less than one (1) hour of high-quality programming a day.
- 2-5 years: one (1) hour of TV, iPad, or video games a day.
- 5+ years: Parents decide how much screen time children get, keeping in mind safety, purpose, and content.

Ummmm, what?! These numbers cannot be accurate. Well, it is the Mayo Clinic, so I'll let you be the judge of their accuracy.

Most children use devices for much longer than these guidelines. Are you feeling some Parent Guilt right now? I know I am. These guidelines could not and would not have worked in my house. Mine felt their lives were boring if they didn't have their devices, almost as if they were deprived of a basic need.

Here is some advice: You must do what works for you and your family to maintain your sanity and for you and your children to get through the day without a major meltdown.

If you are able to adhere to the aforementioned guidelines, then I am in awe. Many of us will have a hard time with these time restrictions. It's OK. Only you know how to run your house best. This is a no guilt, no judgement area. I am just sharing the recommended guidelines.

Junk Food is a Weakness

There is nothing better than a fresh chocolate-chip cookie straight out of the oven or a newly opened bag of potato chips. Can't you taste it right now? Yummmm!

Junk food indulges our mischievous side. It entices us, makes us consume it, and then we feel guilty.

Healthy food that we bring into the house seems to last forever, but any junk food is inhaled at lightning speed.

Well, that is how it happens in my house, at least.

When your child wants to indulge in some yummy, yet unhealthy, junk food, your answer is probably "no" most of the time. If you're like me, you have probably had this conversation a few hundred times. However, there are times when you just don't have the time or energy to debate the merits of a healthy snack vs. junk food.

Many of us cave in and say, "Whatever." Junk food, obviously, has little or no nutritional value, but it is OK for children to have some junk food once in a while. Do not feel guilty if your child occasionally has a bowl of cereal for dinner or cinnamon rolls for breakfast. Everything in moderation is OK, as my mother always tells me. You must bear in mind, though, your heredity, exercise, and health. And always check with your doctor on any health-related or dietary issues.

Also, if you have teenagers and young adults, it is a safe bet they will not eat an apple or banana at 2 a.m. when they are looking for a snack before bed. And you have no idea what they are putting in their mouths when they are out with friends or studying at Starbucks.

Do not feel guilty about things that are not life-altering.

Parent Meltdown, Now What?!

Unless you are a saint, we have all lost our cool with our children. Some stressor has triggered us, and we blow our stack. It could be as simple as a sock lying on the floor.

By default, many of us start yelling to get our children's attention to show how upset we are (guilty). However, it is more likely that our frustration is stemming from a place of fatigue, feeling overwhelmed, or feeling stressed about something that has nothing to do with our children. And yet, they are the recipients of our frustration.

If they are in danger or defiant, then you may need to raise your voice to get their attention. So, as we discussed in the chapter "Take Care of You," putting yourself in a Parent Time-out can be an effective way to diffuse the situation and have the same impact of letting them know that their behavior is unacceptable.

Another quick story:

When I lost my cool with my children, which happened more times than I wish to admit, I had two options:

a. I could dig my heels in and say, "I'm the adult, and you were wrong," which is half true. I am the adult. They may have been incorrect or not. It might have just been my reaction to their behavior. After all, my child doesn't know what I have on my plate, my stress level, or how exhausted I am. *Or,*

b. I could apologize.

Huh? What would I apologize for when my child's behavior caused the meltdown? The action my children displayed may very well have needed to be addressed. But my loud, boisterous reaction to it was not the way to get them to listen to me. It only showed them I was upset, and I was not in a space to have a rational conversation.

My apology was more to let them know that my behavior was unacceptable and out of order, but not what I was frustrated about. I would always caveat it with, "I'm not apologizing for the content of what I was saying because yes, I was upset about X, Y or Z. But I am frustrated that I asked you three times to put your laundry up and you chose not to. And when you didn't put it up after my third request, I became angry, and I've now gone to the dark side."

I am not apologizing for the content. I am apologizing for my delivery. Or: I am apologizing for my RESPONSE to your behavior, NOT your behavior. (Though, honestly, I am not sure most young children would/could make that distinction.)

We are the adults, and we should model what behaviors we want our children to emulate. We feel a lot of guilt when we know we did not react in the right way. We are human and we make mistakes. The key is to apologize and let your children know that you are fallible. This creates trust between you both, and you will feel relief when they hug you and tell you that they accept your apology.

Your Older Children and Parent Guilt

When your children are college-age or even adults with their own families, it becomes harder to carve out time with them. They have their own lives, commitments, and social engagements that take up their days and nights, so scheduling time to be together can become challenging. However, it is just as essential to create memories and have quality time with them at this stage of their lives as when they were younger and still under your roof.

When you go to your parents' home, they likely want to take care of you like they did when you were little. There is something quite calming about being back in your comfort zone with people you know and love. Our older children want to feel the same way. However, there is a new norm now that they are independent and have their own ways of doing things that may clash with your habits and beliefs. So, finding common ground is a must. We have to be willing to accept their independence and freedom while also making sure that they remember it is our house.

The easiest way to accomplish this is to have an honest, open conversation. Ask them what their expectations are. What favorite foods can you make for them? Will they be visiting other family or friends? What activities would they like to do during their visit? You should also be clear as to what your expectations are. Such as which meals you would like them home for and what activities would you like them to participate in.

This open conversation will decrease any uncertainties on either side and allow your children to have some control while they are visiting. Selfishly, we want our children to have a fabulous time, and for them to keep coming back. By having a simple, direct talk, we can alleviate some of our Parent Guilt by having a clearer understanding of the boundaries.

Punam's Perspective

Parent Guilt is real. I don't know one parent who doesn't want to do what's best for their child. But what makes it best? A nutritious meal? Attending all their extracurriculars? Making sure they feel loved?

Honestly, I felt like all of these were and are important with my own children. But it was not always possible. Even today, I constantly feel guilty thinking about what I haven't done for my children—frequently doubting my parenting abilities.

Here is the truth: We have done more than we give ourselves credit for. We always look at what we haven't done, what we should have done, or what is left to do. When we stand back and look at what we *have* accomplished, we probably have completed more than we have not.

So, let's focus on the positive. It's easier to look at the negative, which makes us feel guilty, but that's not a productive or healthy habit. This is the lesson my daughter taught me with a single, positive statement when I was focusing on my perceived failures.

I urge you to focus on reducing your Parent Guilt by turning your energies to all the wonderful things you are doing. It is more beneficial, productive, and healthier for you, your children, and your family.

THREE
GET INVOLVED

Laying a strong, early social, emotional, and academic foundation for your child makes it easier for them to transition from home to school. So, let's shift our conversation into our children's educational years. During our children's schoolyears, we are busy trying to get them ready in the morning, while trying to get ourselves to work, hustling to make it to their extracurriculars, preparing dinner, and then getting ready to do it all over again the next day. It can seem impossible to consider adding one more thing to your plate.

Parenting can be rewarding, challenging, and unpredictable during the "parenting season" of our lives. Many of us are so busy with our daily routines that volunteering at our school seems unthinkable. But a significant predictor of student success is parent involvement in schools—not the caliber of the school or our children's peer group, according to a 2018 article by Centers for Disease Control and Prevention.

But how? I am barely making it through the day. I'm exhausted all the time. I cannot accomplish what I need to, and now you ask me to find time to volunteer in my children's schools?

Well, the short answer is . . . yes.

Here is the longer answer. Parenting is a long game—a marathon, not a sprint. It is likely you will not see any immediate parenting dividends while you are actively raising your children or for that matter, while running long distances. As a long-distance runner myself, who has run four marathons, I can assure you that running long distances, like parenting, requires building stamina, and developing the discipline necessary to build mental and physical strength. But it also requires time, diligence, and perseverance.

Generally, rewards come after lots of hard work and dedication, which can take years in some cases.

Here is the scoop. Our lives are built on relationships. We create a relationship with our bosses to ensure we are on their "good" side and to further our careers. We develop relationships and friendships to ensure we feel confident and secure by surrounding ourselves with like-minded people who can build us up. We have a relationship and bond with our significant other. When we foster those relationships, we learn, grow, are more connected, and become more open in our thoughts. We also begin to understand how systems work, how to work within them, and, if we feel the need, how to be an effective change agent.

Building a relationship with your child's school is precisely the same. By getting to know the teachers and administrators, by understanding the education system, learning how to work within the guidelines set forth by the respective governing agencies, and understanding how we can bring about positive change, we can improve our education system as a whole.

So, how can you become involved?

Show Interest

Expressing interest may seem like a no-brainer when it involves volunteering in schools, but you would be surprised at how many parents show little-to-no interest in their child's school. They leave the education process entirely up to the administration and teachers. Many think, "Teachers know what they are doing, so I don't need to worry about it."

This leads me to believe one of two things: The parent is either intimidated by their lack of understanding of the school system, or their other commitments take priority.

It is important to remember that you know your child and how to best raise them. You know what is happening in their personal lives that may affect their performance in school, and it is your job to help their teachers so they can do the job they are trained to do: teach.

Assisting in your child's education, showing interest in their progress, and building a relationship with their teachers implies that you care about your child's educational outcomes that will build paths for a successful future.

Let's now talk about how to become involved in your child's school.

Engaging in Opportunities

This phrase presents a conundrum. Without engaging in school and supporting the teacher, the opportunities may be sparse or difficult to find. But to create those connections, you need to build relationships, so the opportunities present themselves.

For example, if your child's teacher has seen you around the school, or you have emailed them to keep abreast of what is going on and to let them know how to reach you, then your opportunities for engagement likely increase.

Confused? Don't be.

Teachers are eager to invite parents who show interest in becoming engaged in their classrooms. Those parents who reach out with genuine interest can have real opportunities in the classroom and school.

Here's an idea that can improve your volunteer opportunities. Contact your child's teacher at the beginning of the year. Let them know your availability and interests. If you work full time or your time is limited, be sure to share that information. It's best to follow up with an email detailing what you have discussed, so the teacher has it in writing to refer back to. Also, check-in with the teacher periodically. You can simply send them a short email to ask how your child is doing in class and/or to let them know that you are still available to help them.

Teachers are happy to receive help. They are always overworked and multitasking. They are hungry for good volunteers.

Be a Good Volunteer

Here are a few tips to be a good volunteer.

Be punctual.

- If you are supposed to be there at 8 a.m., be there 10 minutes early. Remember, you still have to sign in, get your badge, and walk to the classroom.
- Make sure you have any materials you are responsible for. The teacher and students are relying on you to be prepared.
- You are there to help the entire class, not only your child.

Do your "job".

- During the activity is not the time to insert yourself to make changes you deem more efficient. Often, teachers repeat the same activity for years, and have perfected a way that works for them. Remember, they are the boss of their classrooms.

Be courteous and gracious.

- If your child is having difficulties with another student, observe and then follow up with the teacher quietly. You cannot make a scene by talking badly about the child to the other students or even the parents.
- Every student is someone's child. If you would not want your child to be spoken ill of, then you must show the same courtesy to others' children.

Ask.

- Where can I help?
- What do you need?
- Can I send some supplies to help?

These are some questions you can ask, even in an email, to help your child's teacher. This can be an excellent way to volunteer if you are a working parent.

Be genuine.

- Here is where the Golden Rule comes in. You know, *Do Unto Others as You Would Have Them*

Do Unto You. Most people can sniff out
disingenuous people a mile away.

- Watch for clues in the behavior of other parent
  volunteers.

Do they talk only about themselves?
Do they think their children are infallible?
Are they oblivious to what is happening around them?

If the answer to any of these is *yes*, I am going to tell you to
RUN! They are looking to advance their own agenda and want
you to help them. That is not what teachers are looking for in
classroom volunteers.

Teachers want authentic helpers who work for the good of
the whole class. They are seeking those individuals who will be
thoughtful, honest, kind, and interested in the activity/event
and the students.

Have fun.

- If you are taking time out of your already busy
  schedule to help, then do yourself and everyone
  else a favor and be happy while you are in the
  school. My graduate school professor once told me
  something that has stuck with me for nearly 30
  years:

Children do not care what burden you are carrying. So,
when you walk through the door of a classroom, leave the burden
there. Savor the time you are spending in the school and inter-
acting with the students. They need to see you enjoying what
you are doing. You can pick up your burden on the way out the
door and go back to your challenges when you leave.

. . .

That piece of advice has stuck with me for decades. And each time I have walked into the school or classroom, I have tried to heed my professor's guidance.

If you need to talk to the teacher:

- You cannot barge into the school and classroom to air your grievance about something that has happened to your child. If you do not condone bullying, then do not be one. It's pretty simple.
- Email the teacher and set up an appointment convenient to all parties if you need to chat.
- Take a deep breath before speaking. Remember that the teacher, who spends time with your child, is responsible for teaching them, and needs to feel that they are not being judged harshly by your conversation.
- Be solution-oriented. Once you have aired your grievance, focus on the solutions. It is helpful to have thought of a few possible options before the meeting.
- Be respectful.

I know I am sharing the obvious here, but this is your friendly reminder.

But wait! I work full time, and I don't have time to be in my child's classroom. I haven't forgotten about you. I promise. We just needed to get through the basics first.

Working Parents

Hats off to you! Working full time is no joke. It is an additional layer of stress and responsibility added to your life.

How can you be engaged in your child's school when you have the added pressure of a job? According to Neelam Chakrabarty, CEO and co-founder of Oroola, schools and parent organizations need to increase parental involvement. By addressing the challenges many working parents face, such as time constraints, lack of motivation, lack of knowledge about the educational process, and language barriers, schools and parent organizations can proactively reach out to help offset these barriers to create a cohesive team.

Working parents have many opportunities to engage in schools, depending on what the school's needs are. The first task, though, is to look at your calendar and determine your availability. In fact, this goes for ALL parents. Second, reach out to the teacher or event organizer to let them know your times and availability after checking your calendar. Be realistic in your ability to commit to the school. It is much better to under-commit and over-deliver.

Here are some ways working parents can become involved:

- Pick the activity/event you would like to participate in and volunteer. You may choose to take time off work, use your lunch break, or select events at times that do not conflict with your work. But if it is important for you to be in attendance for events that feature your child, then one of these could be an option.

- Schools may have evening events to accommodate working families. This could be your ticket!
- Ask the teacher or organizer if there is anything you can do from home. For example:

Can you make phone calls to round up some volunteers?
Can you prepare anything for the activity/event?
Can you send any supplies, snacks, or money to offset the class-room costs?
Can you come in before or after school to help if your schedules allow?

These are some options that will give you flexibility to volunteer. Again, teachers are always looking for willing and consistent volunteers who follow through, are kind to their students, and do not make a fuss. Be that person. Building relationships (there is that word again: relationship) is the foundation of it all. By building a trusting relationship, being genuine, and showing interest, you can become a tremendous ally for your child and the school.

Punam's Perspective

When I decided to stay home after my first child was born, most of my days in the early years were taking care of the house and family. As she grew older and started school, I decided to volunteer in her schools. Increasingly, I would volunteer more when opportunities and time permitted. But remember, I still had three children at home when my oldest began kinder-garten. I kept telling myself that this was a marathon and I needed to pace myself in order to be a consistent and effective volunteer. I knew I had a long way to go in raising the kids, so my volunteer time needed to accommodate our family's schedule. After all, that is why I was staying at home in the first place.

Within a few years, when all my children were in school, my volunteer time became more flexible. I began volunteering for anything and everything I could. It helped me emotionally to be near my children. It was also a new avenue to pursue my passion for education without having to deal with the systemic bureaucracy I had encountered as a teacher. Soon, without realizing it, I was welcomed in their schools doing various activities almost every day.

How did I get to that point? I worked on building relationships without regard as to whether they would create volunteer opportunities—though it certainly did indeed do that. Getting to know the teachers who were spending time with my children was important. I began my volunteering career in the media center. Teachers could help me understand my children's needs and I was learning more objective approaches as they guided me. I trusted their opinions, and they, for the most part, trusted mine. Soon, in addition to my time in the media center, I was starting to find myself in more leadership roles at the school-wide level in addition to my time in the classroom.

Who knew this was going to be my calling?

When my children began their middle and high school careers, one of my observations was that when children are at this this stage of their academics, it is unusual to have a lot of parental involvement in their schools. Somehow, it's become accepted that parents do not need to be involved when their children get older. The thought must be that the students and teachers are OK since there are no holiday parties, honor roll parties, or other celebrations that we typically see in the elementary classrooms.

There was a small group of us parents who, when our children reached high school, continued to volunteer to be connected. When my children were in high school, I knew my children's teachers and would email, call, and consult them throughout the year.

Here was my logic: by the time they are in high school, they are beginning to spend more time with friends without parental oversight. It is the place where children are most likely exposed to all kinds of new things.

In my mind, I wanted to know who my children were hanging out with. I began to realize that parents need to be *most* involved in high school albeit in different ways. I learned that it is important to know who their friends are, observe their interactions without interfering, and to monitor how well they are adjusting to their new-found freedoms and responsibilities. This allowed me to provide guidance and help them cope should issues arise. Get to know the teachers and other parents. By doing so, you build those relationships and friendships where you can help each other as you navigate parenting during this potentially challenging period of their lives.

Volunteering is what I did for almost 20 years. I knew every teacher and what subject they taught and made lasting friends with so many that I have their contact information in my phone —even though my children may have been in their class over 20 years ago.

Here are my tricks:

- The teachers became my friends. I have many wonderful memories with them.
- I never took them for granted.
- We always took each other at our word.
- I talked with my children frequently about what was happening in their classrooms.
- I never was aggressive or belligerent when speaking

to teachers and administrators.

- There were three teachers in the entire time my four children were in public schools that I made a fuss over because I felt they were not a good fit for my child.

My philosophy was to demonstrate to my children that when they got out into the working world, their boss or co-workers might also be difficult people. My children needed to learn how to develop coping skills. But the three times I felt that my children were being mistreated, I stood up for them. And because I had built relationships with the faculty and staff and did not go into the conference as a bully, my concerns were met with understanding and compassion.

Building relationships is essential. We do so with our significant other, our friends, family, and colleagues. Relationships with our children's teachers are just as crucial as any other relationship that we spend time developing. The more our children's school experiences are positive, the more likelihood of success. The more they feel confident and secure, the more likely they will be inspired to continue to achieve.

It's not always easy to carve out time to volunteer because of our busy schedules. But the outcome—the success and the confidence you afford your child by volunteering—can be one of the most beneficial effects on your child that will last a lifetime. Consider reaching out to your child's teacher and school. The impact that you have as a volunteer on a child's academic career may never fully be known. But I promise you, it will be vast and everlasting.

"Be the change you wish to see in the world."
–Gandhi

FOUR

READ, READ AND READ SOME MORE

The more that you read,
the more things you will know.
The more things you learn,
the more places you will go.
–Dr. Seuss

This is one of my all-time favorite quotes to promote reading. Dr. Seuss was a wise man who brilliantly weaved life lessons for everyone into all of his children's books. So, when parents read to their children, they also receive pearls of wisdom to reflect upon and instill in their own lives. We all know reading is an integral part of a child's success in school and beyond. But what impact does reading actually have on your child? Well, let's start at the beginning.

J. Richard Gentry, Ph.D., an author, educator and speaker, advocates for parents to start reading to their child when they are young (think in-utero, newborns, and infants). He shared this with my audience on my podcast, edu-Me—a podcast that focuses on bridging the gap to foster a stronger relationship between parents and schools by empowering parents to become partners in their child's education.

By doing so, your child hears words, begins relating them in context, and creates visions and beliefs about the world. It sounds crazy to think children can learn at such a young age. But as Dr. Gentry shared, a parent who has read to their child throughout their youngest years will enter kindergarten having heard 30 million more words than a child who has not had the same opportunity. 30 *million*! An astounding number, right!? I almost fell out of my chair when he shared this information. In his book, *Brain Words: How the Science of Reading Informs Teaching,* co-written with Gene P. Ouellette, Ph.D., they convincingly present these facts and additional research revealing that children who are read to in their early years are more successful throughout their lives.

But as with any successful process, there are always challenges:

- How do we create strong readers?
- How much do we read to our children?
- How will I know that I am creating a strong reader?
- I get bored doing the same activity. What can I do?

You must start reading to them when they are born. Young children cannot read to you, so you are the one in charge of making sure you read to them. I found that reading to my children just before bedtime was the easiest. Everyone was winding down and relaxing. The house was "closed" for the night, and it was an easy segue to bedtime. (We discuss this further under **Read Alouds.**) There are some fun, exciting ways to encourage reading as children get older. You have likely seen or heard of many of these. But here are some practical solutions to squeezing in reading time. As a reminder, these are suggestions. You should implement a reading routine that works for you and your family.

Book Clubs

Book Clubs were revived several years ago when Oprah Winfrey created one and resurrected the love of reading for so many. Women, in particular, would read the books she recommended and then get together with wine and hors d'oeuvres to discuss the book while having an evening away from the family. You can apply the same principle (with sparkling grape juice) with your children. Pick a book—maybe one they are required to read at school, a favorite of theirs, or one on a topic that piques their interests—and read it. Once you have both finished the book, you can set up a time where you can discuss it while enjoying your favorite snacks.

Jennifer Thompson, a reading specialist from Manassas Public County Schools in Virginia, says, "Book clubs are so appealing because children can truly get lost in a book without standardized tests looming, no comprehension questions to answer, just the pure satisfaction of reading for enjoyment." In other words, book clubs help make the independent act of reading into a social activity.

Book clubs check several boxes while encouraging your child to read:

- Your child has read a book. (yay!)
- You have read a book. (double yay!)
- You have created a fun way to connect with your child.

- You are making memories with them that will last a lifetime.

Read Alouds

As mentioned earlier, I read to my children when they were young and unable to read by themselves. This was our last snuggle-time before bed. It was my opportunity to close the day by curling up with the most important people in my life. Read Alouds are such a fun way to create independent readers while still getting to snuggle with your little one.

However, when they became older, around two-years-old, I allowed them to "read" to me. They could pick their favorite book and "read" the words. In the beginning, they were not reading, of course. They were mimicking what they saw and heard because this is how we learn behaviors. They were creating a story by looking at the pictures on the page. Oh, how entertaining those stories were!

It is fun and exciting to hear them read, make up their own words, create their own stories, and share them. These are the beginnings of a developing reader. Read Alouds give children validation and boost their self-esteem and confidence in public speaking—two crucial skills needed for academic success. When they have heard the story innumerable times, they begin to recite the story from memory. This is another critical step in your child's progression to becoming an independent reader. As they learn the alphabet and begin to string the letters into words, they begin to sound out the words in the book, and they are finally able to read by themselves. That is a momentous day. You have a reader on your hands!

Reflections

Being reflective is a powerful learning tool. There is so much to learn from contemplating a specific day or event—how did we react and what we can do better? It is also an impactful way to share your history with others. We all have events in our lives that have shaped us, whether they are positive or not. Regardless of whether it happened because *of* us or *to* us, there is a story to tell.

We will discuss reflections in two parts. One idea is journaling, where you pen your thoughts, ideas, and emotions down in a private, semi-private, or even public forum. We discussed this in the chapter, *Take Care of Yourself*, but we are now using that same premise with our children. The nice part about journaling is that you have control over how much you share, if any at all, with the outside world. Your journal entries can touch on whatever topic moves you at that moment. They are your own unique thoughts.

Julie Axelrod, in her 2016 article shares some of her ideas which are intertwined with my own below.

Encouraging your children to journal can be beneficial in many ways.

- Children begin to understand the power of the pen and how words can impact the outcome of their lives.
- Journaling helps children pinpoint their emotions, ask for help if needed, and learn coping mechanisms more effectively.
- Children verbally communicate more effectively and more succinctly once they have vetted their thoughts on paper.
- Journaling helps children prioritize their emotions

and helps them decide which ones need immediate attention.

The second idea is also a type of journaling—a recording of reflections—but in a different way. Our parents and grandparents have had experiences we can never imagine. They experienced wars, social-justice issues, and personal successes and struggles. Your child can "interview" them and record the dialogue on a cell phone or any other recording device as they listen to their family member describe their life's journey.

Chronicling these events for your family members offers valuable insight as to how those historical events, as well as personal events, affected and shaped their lives. The bonus is that you will likely have some type of biography to share with the rest of the family and a treasured piece of history for generations to come. How awesome would that be?

Your Own Story

While we are discussing chronicling stories, how about a story your child creates from her or his own imagination? Children have vivid "make-believe engines" and can make up the liveliest stories. Why not record them and then, one day, turn them into a book of short stories? It would be such a keepsake for them. And who knows, they could become a published author!

Since we have easy access to recording and writing devices — computers, tablets, phones, etc. — let's put them to good use to chronicle our families' most impactful stories.

When I Find Myself in Times of Trouble

Are you hearing Paul McCartney singing in your head yet? When you listen to these classic Beatles song lyrics, you hear hope and yearning for a better future, one where whatever currently ails you is now manageable, and you believe there will be a positive outcome.

If a child is facing a troubling time, whether at home, at school or due to other factors, they are likely searching for some sign of hope. Fairytales are a great way to share hope with children. Think back to your favorite fairytales: *Hansel and Gretel, Puss in Boots, The Ugly Duckling*, or any other favorite. The main characters face some challenge that leaves you wondering how they will overcome it, and yet, they do. They use their power, strength, and determination to overcome the barrier placed in their paths. There is a positive outcome for the hero at the end of every fairytale—good triumphs over evil. Fear is mitigated by hope—calm overcomes stresses—and we live happily ever after.

In times of uncertainty, fairytales can bring the hope that children are looking for. Everyone wants to believe a stressful time will end in a positive manner, especially children. Reading them can bring reassurance and the calm children are searching for. It helps them to know everything will be OK.

My Child Can Read But Will Not

Aaah, the old excuse, "I do not know how to!" line. Boy, children learn this one early, don't they? And trust me, they will continue to use this into their adulthood! If you feel confident your child should be reading, and we are primarily speaking of Pre-K/Kindergarten children here, there could be a few factors preventing this. They may not be developmentally ready to read. Every child matures at a different time, and reading is one skill children must be developmentally ready for.

Or they do not want to miss the thrill/comfort of snuggling with you while you read a book. We may be eager for our child to be an independent reader, but our children innately understand that they will lose that undivided time with you if they showcase their reading skills. They could feel some separation anxiety, so I am surmising that they may be "choosing" not to read in your presence.

So, if you want them to show you they can read, do some role reversal. Allow children to choose a book that you feel confident they would know how to read. The story they choose doesn't matter. They may be reading it from memory. That's OK. Reading occurs in many ways and all of us, initially, memorize the letters and formation of words to read. Children are doing the same thing. It is the normal progression toward becoming an independent reader.

Here is another trick I used when my children were little: While I was reading a story, I would purposefully change a word, sentence, or add something absurd in there to see: a) if they were paying attention and, b) to see if they knew what the word or sentence should be. Children will usually laugh and call you out, but it is a useful tool to ensure your child comprehends what you are reading.

Art Comes to Life

I dream my painting and then paint my dream.
–Vincent Van Gogh

Many of us have seen a play or musical. Whether it is a school performance or on Broadway, these performances engross you with their stories. The stories are told through an art form, the performing arts.

Most children love art. They love to perform, sing, dance, color, paint, or draw. Art helps form many aspects of your child's development, from creating a balance between the left brain and right brain to refining the gross/fine motor skills. Whether it is music, visual arts, dance, or another medium conducive to your family, art can have a life-altering impact on your life.

With this in mind, how can we bring art and reading together? Once you have read a book, you can paint a scene from the book, create a piece of music representing the book's tone and mood, or dance a scene from the book. These are just some ideas. Engaging children in reading through art forms is a perfect way to encourage reading and develop a love of art.

Punam's Perspective

As you can tell, I am a huge advocate for reading. As a child of educators and an educator myself, the importance of reading was instilled in me at a very early age, and I have passed it on to my children.

As a bilingual person, I have learned to read in English and my parents' native language, Hindi (which is my first language). By reading in both languages, I have broadened my views of the world, begun to understand various perspectives, and learned to stay excited about reading.

So, you can imagine how important it was for our family to celebrate any book that my children enjoyed or that stretched their imaginations or understanding of the world. Reading can become routine and boring if we do not create exciting ways to keep our children motivated. And there are so many ways to make reading fun, especially for those children who do not love to read. Each of my four children has a love of reading, but their passion levels vary.

My children are adults now, and some read voraciously about all kinds of topics, and others stick to their interests. Either way, they are reading and expanding their knowledge base. My goal was to ensure they enjoyed reading enough to keep reading and not have it feel like a task.

We now have book clubs within our own home and enjoy discussing the books together. Their points of view are invariably different than mine; we are all learning from each other. As long as reading is exciting and enjoyable for your child, I consider it a win!

So, start early, give your children a head start, and begin creating strong readers!

FIVE

THE IMPACT OF TESTING

Note: The phrases "high-stakes testing" and "state-mandated testing" will be used interchangeably in this chapter. Although high-stakes testing can also describe other tests like the SAT, ACT, or GRE, this chapter focuses on mandated testing at the individual school level.

Hearing the word "test" brings a shiver up many of our spines. We hear the word, and we immediately feel tense and anxious, and possibly even conjure up some PTSD from our own childhood testing experiences.

Now that we are the parents, how do we approach the issue of academic testing for our children? We want them to be successful. The stakes do seem higher today, and without strong grades and test scores, our children's post-secondary plans may be at risk.

Let's hit the *"pause"* button here to identify the two types of testing we discuss in this chapter.

Mastery of Skills/Comprehension Testing

- These are the assessments our children are given
  frequently in various subjects. They take the form
  of weekly tests, chapter tests, and the like. Our
  children have many tests like these throughout the
  academic year.

Standardized Testing

- These tests are given infrequently with higher
  stakes attached to them. Promotion/retention and
  class placement are just two of the "stakes" or
  consequences these tests determine concerning our
  children's academic paths.

"Unpause:" If your children's school was like my children's,
it seemed they had some type of test every time we turned
around. In fact, testing is so frequent that it's hard to keep up
with it all. Whether it is a weekly spelling test, a chapter test in
history, or the SAT, testing was a weekly event.

And a weekly stressor.

There is so much pressure to achieve more and more and
score higher and higher. Test scores can impact grade promotion, class rank, and, often, the self-confidence of a child. Never
mind the core reason for testing: mastery of a set of skills, and
equally important, identifying those skills that need more
attention.

But what is the purpose of testing? Why do schools test
incessantly?

Mastery Level Testing

The initial purpose of testing was to ensure students were learning the skills taught to them with some level of comprehension and to assess a degree of mastery. The state or district gave teachers the concepts they were required to teach for each grade level (the standards), and the teachers would create the curriculum, lessons, and tests to ensure that students were attaining an acceptable level of understanding.

Many, *many* years ago, when I was teaching in an elementary school, I learned how important it was to develop the understanding of the basics of a subject before building on more complex skills. Testing provides student data that teachers can utilize as they move forward in their planning process. It is not much different today, but the emphasis then was more on classroom teaching and testing as opposed to standardized assessments at various grade levels.

While testing for skills still occurs today, teachers are often told precisely how and when to teach a particular skill. This allows the school district (and the parents) to know that every seventh-grade math teacher, for example, is teaching the same skill at the same time. It brings a level of homogeneity to teaching and promotes collaboration between teachers across the schools and the district. It also ensures that every child is receiving equal time on the concepts.

Similar to testing in schools today, we also took an annual state test, e.g., a high-stakes test. When I was in school, these tests were given to provide the administration and teachers feedback—whether the instruction had been successful or not. These tests were used more as an evaluative tool and not as heavily weighted with academic consequences as they are today. For example, children may or may not be promoted based on their scores. Or they can be placed in a class solely focused on providing remediation to increase their understanding of the subject. Additionally, these classes can impact the students' schedules, potentially eliminating certain courses (like art or music classes) from their school day.

Testing Season

Testing Season is what we called it in my house when the state-mandated, high-stakes tests were administered. It is the most dreaded, stressful time of the year for many homes—the time when all discussions revolve around the next set of tests. A significant portion of the school year is devoted to ensuring each student in the state has been tested. In Florida, where my children went to school, it took almost two months to administer all the relevant tests.

Understanding the importance of these tests, for both students and teachers, becomes necessary to prepare students well in advance. Teachers spend a tremendous amount of time preparing students with those skills, ensuring they have been exposed to the subject matter that they will be tested on. Therefore, there is a LOT of time focused on testing.

So, when your child is stressed out about this test, there is a good reason. The stakes can be high.

High-Stakes Testing Complexity

State administered tests have high stakes attached to student success. They are a beast unto themselves. These tests vary from state to state. The various State Departments of Education create the tests, the schedules, and then pay someone to grade them. The administration of these tests varies from state to state, as well. From this, you can also conclude that the outcomes vary, too. These tests affect the student's educational path. It is a long and arduous process to ensure that each child is tested in the most conducive environment for optimal success.

As discussed in the previous section, testing, especially state testing, takes months to complete. It is incredibly stressful for the faculty and staff and students. What can parents do to help them? What impact does this have on them?

Here are some ways we, as parents, can help our children cope with the stress of testing and help them be as successful as possible.

We can:

- Talk to them
- Help them understand the significance of the test
- Keep their spirits high and positive
- Provide healthy meals
- Let them know it's going to be OK

The Positives of Testing/Assessment

There are positives to testing and frequent assessments. Testing can provide vital information for:

- Determining how well the curriculum is delivered
- Determining how the teacher is teaching
- Determining how well the students are grasping the concepts
- Determining how well students are doing compared to their peers

This is crucial data for educators and Departments of Education to understand so they can make adjustments, if necessary, to the curriculum and/or instructional strategies to ensure student success. In fact, Carly Berwick, teacher and journalist, shares that testing can provide feedback, increase retrieval of content, and determine where teachers need to reteach the skills for mastery. Thus, testing and assessment does have a legitimate place in organized schooling.

Each of these skills is important for preparing for the post-secondary world in addition to the work-world. Our children need some mastery of academic skills for them to be successful in the workforce. But how can we walk the fine line of ensuring our children have the skills necessary to be successful and protect them from the stress and anxiety that testing brings?

How Do Tests Impact Our Children?

When I was teaching, I saw many students struggle and even have panic attacks over these tests. They would freeze as soon as the test was placed on their desks.

Students who have test anxiety or low self-confidence realize they have an uphill battle when it comes to these tests. That anxiety can be crippling and can manifest itself into the student not believing in their abilities and potentially not performing well. Tests can bring about a level of stress and anxiety in our children that is detrimental to building self-confidence. They understand the educational and social ramifications of their scores. Children know that others will be watching them and judging them if there is a change in their educational path.

This is a heartbreaking situation. But this is where parental guidance and support are needed.

What Can Parents Do to Help Their Child?

For your child to do their best on these tests, there are some things you can do to set them up for a successful day. Parents can talk to their children about the long-term impact of a particular test. Is it something that will permanently affect their future, like the SAT or ACT? Or is it a chapter test that is testing their knowledge of material taught in a class?

By using this mindset, parents can relieve some of their child's anxiety. Telling them how you feel about the test helps them understand the magnitude of it and its outcome. If you are not worried, then they probably will not be either.

Your child needs to see that you are confident in their abilities. They want to know that you are proud of them, even when, and especially when, they do not feel so. What happens, though, when we know the outcome of a test is important? When the test requires your child to be fully focused? How do we ensure we are giving our children every advantage to have a calm, positive approach to their test?

This is not always easy to figure out, but parents should try to make them as relaxed as possible and send them to school feeling positive and in a good mood. But how?

Here are some suggestions:

- The morning of the test, give your child the positive reinforcement they need to get through the day. Make sure that you are happy and positive with them, especially on those testing days, even if your child is not.
- Tell them that you are proud of them regardless of the score on this test.
- Make their favorite breakfast even if you have to

wake up 30 minutes earlier to do so. It will start
their day off on a good note.
- If your child is not feeling well on testing day, send
  your teacher an email and ask what the options are.

*Sometimes the teacher will say to keep your child home until
they feel better, and they will schedule your child's test on the
makeup day.*

*Sometimes, the teacher will ask the parent to bring the student
in for the part of the school day that is not focused on testing.*

Sometimes, the teacher will say to let them go ahead and test.

Ultimately, though, it is your decision as the parent.

Those testing days, even though stressful at school, can be
relaxing and fun at home. Family time that is fun and relaxing
will change the setting and everyone's mood in the house.

In short, find some balance in your approach to testing—
whatever that looks like.

Punam's Perspective

I have a love/hate relationship with testing. I can see both sides
of the coin and am often torn by the pros and cons. I continue
to struggle with it, even though I am beyond that stage now that
my children are in college.

As an educator, I appreciate the significance of testing and
how it helps teachers tailor their lessons to ensure students
develop mastery of skills. It is the job of the educator to make
certain our students learn these important concepts and
achieve a satisfactory level of proficiency.

But I have empathy for those students who struggle with tests, especially the high-stakes ones, when I know that their scores would not necessarily reflect their actual knowledge of the subject at hand. Watching their anxiety and frustration is challenging and painful.

Unfortunately, though, we live in a testing world where metrics measure us. Tests carry over into our careers, even though our work "tests" may look differently.

When I became a parent, how I approached testing with my children was formed from my teaching experience. I have seen my children's anxiety on test day and the worries that overwhelmed them when they thought they could not do well. And I worried about what the impact of their educational path would be if they didn't do well.

My children are divided when it comes to testing. Two of them take tests in stride and say, "I've got this, and whatever score I get is awesome." The other two are anxious and nervous about the tests and the resulting scores. Although they all did OK, no, very well, it was nerve-wracking for the entire family when they all took tests on the same day. But on those testing days, I used the strategies outlined above, and I also shared this with them:

It is one test. One test does not define you.

One test does not change who you are.

Your doing well on this test has no bearing on what your success will be in the future.

I said this year, after year, after year. My children could probably recite this from memory even today.

Did I fudge the truth a bit? Well, yes, a bit. The test does define their immediate academic track and what type of classes they might be placed in for the next academic year. It may even impact their "street cred" with their peer group. But it did not and does not bear any weight on what their future looks like. You can fail a test and still be successful. Go figure!

Even when my children became teenagers and were looking at their post-secondary plans, they still faced the anxiety of testing. Whether it was a state test, SAT, or GRE, it was all stressful. But our job, as parents, is to help them understand that it is just a test. Yes, just a test. And you may not do well on it, but it's not the end of the world.

In fact, not doing well on a test every so often is not a bad thing. Sometimes that failure is exactly what is needed to re-energize yourself to get yourself back on track. Life is full of challenges, and we need to develop skills to pick ourselves back up. Just because you have test anxiety or do not do well on a test does not mean you are doomed for life. And just because you do well on the test does not mean you will become a millionaire. Often, there is no direct parallel that can be drawn between these two paths. According to, "Good Grades Don't Guarantee Professional Success," children may be in search of more creativity in schools or a different way of understanding concepts and skills. The test itself becomes limiting in how they express their curiosity about the world around them.

Anecdote: Think of Steve Jobs. He did not graduate from college, but he transformed the world with his vision of the iPhone and other Apple products. Not all of us should be or will be a Steve Jobs, but his story is an example of how someone took their innate abilities and visions and used them to make the world more connected.

Testing is bureaucratic in many ways. The clients are our children. We should be catering to them. To make sure they are happy and confident in their work and give them every tool to succeed and to ensure that our client is "profitable."

We often don't do that for many students. They get lost in the bureaucratic shuffle in the game of states and districts to make money. And those are the children I worry about the most.

But we can be the voice of reason for our children and let them know that testing is the tiniest part of who they are.

And, yes, one test does not define them.

SIX

SOCIAL MEDIA AND YOUR CHILD

If you were born before the mid-1970s, you did not grow up with the craziness of computers, phones, apps, or the ease of access to all that is now online. In the '80s, when I was a teenager, the most exciting thing we had (technology-wise) was the game Pong on Atari. I would play for hours (and boy, was that ball fast!). Since this was one of the first video games, it was exciting to play on this novel device instead of the board games we had grown up with.

The next game we purchased was Pac-Man. Oh my goodness, I was hooked! These games were designed for kids to spend countless hours in front of a screen. Then the best thing happened. My parents bought a Tandy 2000. It was our first computer from Radio Shack, and it was awesome. I could type all my papers, edit them on the monitor, and print them out on our dot matrix printer. (If you have no idea what I am talking about, Google it!) Who knew that these games would evolve into the time-sucking, money-evaporating phenomenon they have become today? As the years have passed, computers and social media have become a constant part of our daily lives.

Social media is a term no one could have imagined in my younger days. Our social media was the evening news for 30 minutes (before the advent of the 24-hour news cycle—I told you I'm old!) and the daily newspaper. There was no Twitter, Facebook, Instagram, or TikTok. It was unfathomable to think these platforms could have existed back then.

But as technology evolved, devices became more readily available, and the Internet developed into yesteryear's Encyclopedia Britannica (again, Google this if you need to). Access to all kinds of information is now immediately available at our fingertips. We never need to leave our chair, sofa, or bed to find whatever our hearts desire.

It is truly remarkable to think how far information technology has advanced in less than a generation. Those of us who grew up before the 1980s have had a tremendous learning curve as we try to stay relevant and engage in this relatively new tech-savvy world that we live in. Some of us are still struggling to type a document in Word. (Guilty!) So, bear with me as I share my social media assessment and its ramifications for our children.

Generations Y and Z

[Where are Generations A-W? Did we skip them? Have we exhausted the English alphabet since the next generation is called Alpha? Are we now moving to Greek letters? We used to name generations—"The Greatest Generation" or "Baby Boomers"—but now we have letters.

These are just some of the random thoughts that go through my head. Anyway, I am *way* off-topic]

These children have never known a life without computers, mobile phones, or social media. Apps are usually, especially for children, full of colors, animation, and music to captivate their attention. Embedded in these wonderfully mesmerizing apps are lessons that are being taught without children even realizing it. They quickly learn to use the web's infinite access, along with software tools like PowerPoint and Audacity. Since they are metaphorically born into this medium, they intuitively use these devices and have no difficulty communicating with others through social apps. They send texts, SnapChats, and Instagram stories, to name a few. These seem to be the current communication method (although, in actuality, there may be a new method by the time you're reading this).

Since children have access to this information and can easily navigate it, social media can be difficult for parents to monitor, especially if you have not grown up with it or are technically challenged when it comes to the World Wide Web.

There is also a risk component to social media. Those with nefarious motives have easier access to children and can cause them irreparable harm. While information technology provides an unprecedented opportunity for our children to learn, we certainly cannot ignore the fact that it has potentials of inflicting great harm.

So, let us discuss them head-on.

What Can I Do to Keep My Child Safe?

Before we dive into the details of how to keep them safe, we need to understand that, as *Psychology Today* reports, "tweens [have an] underdeveloped cortex [that] can't manage the distractions nor the temptations that come with social media use...And the longer parents [can] delay access, the more time a child will have to mature so that he or she can use technology more wisely as a young adult."

If social media is new to your repertoire, you must learn the platforms your children are perusing. It's not easy for us to learn and it comes with growing pains, but for your child's safety and security, it is worth the time it will take you to learn the basics of these platforms and to screen specific content. Here are some things you should consider:

- Talk to your children about the boundaries you deem vital to keep them safe.
- Let them be a part of the conversation. Listen to their thoughts and create rules that work for both of you. If they have one idea that you can incorporate, then do so. They will be more likely to follow the rules if they have had some say in them.
- If they can only talk with people they know, then let them know.
- If they cannot go on specific sites without your permission, let them know.
- If they are accessing information that you find harmful or unsafe, tell them. Children must understand their boundaries. Of course, they will test these limitations, but that is where you come in as the parent and need to remind them of the perils of social media.
- Make sure you are monitoring their phones, especially when they are young and going through their teenage years.
- Monitor their texts and any other communication apps they may be using. It is important to check who they are talking to and make sure no cyberbullying is occurring.
- You can do this in a non-threatening way by having a central phone-charging station in the house where you can check their phones. Now for all of you thinking, "That is an invasion of

privacy," well, yes, it is. But when children are young, your job is to protect them from dangerous situations. Children are too young and too naïve to understand all that is available to them on the web, so checking their devices is a protective measure.

- Follow them on the social media platforms they are frequenting to see what they are posting and who they are communicating with.

This is an effective tool to prevent them from engaging in behaviors they know are unacceptable to you.

As a rule of thumb, ask them when they are posting to consider how their grandparents or other well-respected family members will react if they saw their post. Would they be proud of them?

If the answer is no, then your child should reconsider posting it.

This can also keep some of their controversial thoughts out of the public eye.

These are just some ideas for you to consider as your child navigates the wide, wide world of social media.

What Happens if They do not Follow Your Rules

Rules are made to be broken, right? Think back to your younger days and how many rules you broke. We will not discuss mine here, but we have all pushed the boundaries of what our parents felt was safe. Our children are no different in pushing these boundaries, except the consequences of a harmful social media experience can be exponentially more dangerous. So, it's of utmost importance to do all we can to keep our children safe and make sure they abide by the rules we have set.

The consequences of breaking social media, phone, or Internet rules can be the same as breaking any other rule in the house. Or different, depending on the severity of the violation.

Below is a list of potential consequences.

Taking away their phones.

- This seems to be the most popular way to show children the consequences of their social media transgressions.
- It is easy because the device is what created the issue in the first place.
- But, here is a different point of view. At least in our home, we purchased phones for the convenience of communicating with them in case of a schedule change, an emergency, or any other information that needed to be shared. If you take the phone away, then you have cut off that connection and the ability to share information as it may be necessary. Instead, think of alternative ways to send the same message.

Talk to children directly about their offense and give them the chance to explain their decision.

- Use this time as a teaching moment for your children to learn how to have a conversation in which they share their opinion and allow them to explain their actions, which is a great life lesson.
- You do not have to agree with their point of view. But you should respect them enough to listen.

- Share your point of view in terms they can understand. For example, explain why their behavior is dangerous and what the outcomes could be. This will give them a better understanding of social media's potential negative impact and why you are reacting in a certain way.

Let them keep their phones while they are away from the house, but when they get home for the day, ask them to put their phone in the kitchen or some other place away from their sight and reach.

- This way, they are unable to use their phones for the purpose of socialization or playing games. Of course, they are able to access these platforms on their computers, so you need to address those also. If you have a laptop or desktop computer that can be relocated to a central part of the house, then do so, making it available for schoolwork only. This will prevent any use of social media or games during any unsupervised time.
- Children are less likely to veer from your expectations if they know someone may unexpectedly walk by and see what they are doing.

Put parental controls on their phones so they are unable to access those sites that may be dangerous.

- This is an excellent thing to do before you give them the phone. But if you have not and feel the need to, now is the time for you to do so.

Model what you want your children to "put out in the universe."

- As we discussed earlier, if you post something, make sure your children, parents, or grandparents would be proud.
- Always think about how someone else may respond to your post.
- Is it offensive or divisive?
- If we tell our children not to post such thoughts, then we, too, must not post. It's not easy, but we have to be held accountable as well.

When Do You Stop Monitoring their Social Media?

This is one of those "figure it out as you go" deals. Building trust is the key foundation of every relationship. Parents and children must build trust to maintain a strong, healthy, and positive relationship. Your children may be doing well on social media, and you allow them to have a bit more freedom and privacy. They have earned that right. But, if a house rule is broken, it is a privilege that can just as easily be taken away.

Children should still be monitored, though. Monitoring is an integral part of the process to ensure they are staying safe. You can do this by going to their pages from your page. It is an easy way to watch them without "watching" them.

So, the real answer to this question is: I'm not certain that we ever stop monitoring our children. It is built into our parent DNA. Our job is to protect them—always.

Punam's Perspective

Raising four children in the age of social media was a challenge for three reasons:

1. I had no idea how to navigate social media when they first got their phones.
2. Every time there was a new SM platform, I was back at square one trying to figure it out.
3. It is overwhelming to learn a new platform when you have so many other things to manage.

As my children began using social media, I was the overbearing mom who monitored who they were connecting with and what sites they were browsing. If you asked them, they would likely say that I was a crazy, controlling mom, which is probably not far from the truth.

I was terrified, having watched the news of how social media had altered families' lives forever. And there was no precedent on how to parent through this as our generation is the trailblazer, if you will, of parenting children with social media.

So, the tips I have shared with you are all ones I have used in my own home with my own children. In a feeble attempt to keep up with them, I opened an account on all the social media platforms I knew they were on. Our rule was that I had to be one of their friends.

As you can imagine, that was not a popular request. It was met with lots of eye-rolling, "Whys," and "Do you *have tos*?" While I am a people-pleaser by nature, I was not when it came to social media. They had no choice but to be my "friend." I frequently checked to see what my children and their friends were posting. I wanted to make sure they were having healthy, positive conversations.

When there is something new to learn, I usually dive in deeply to see what it is all about. It's my way of getting a more thorough understanding of the concept. I also begin to figure out how to set boundaries for a particular app or platform. These boundaries are in place for the primary reason of keeping children safe. So, when my children posted negative, controversial comments, I would walk into their rooms, close the door, and have a conversation, which usually led to them taking their posts down.

Invariably, they would ask, "Why?" Here is that teaching moment we discussed earlier. Many of my conversations started with, "How do you think your grandmother would feel if she read that?" "Do you think that is a positive reflection of who you are?" "If one of your friends wrote that, how would you feel?"

If any of these answers were negative, my argument was that it should be taken down.

My children would give their best defense as to why they wrote the post. "Because Johnny did this to me, I feel like I should say this" or "My friend was hurt when Susie said that to them, so she deserves to see how it feels to hurt someone." These are predictable responses to some negative actions. And in the mind of a child (and arguably even some adults), these are legitimate reasons to post your feelings.

There has always been a back-and-forth discussion with my children when it comes to social media. As with almost everything, our views change, our knowledge-base changes, and our children open our minds as they try to educate us.

As mine have become young adults and are beginning to find their voices, some of my children's posts give me pause. They do not voice their thoughts in the same manner (nor should they) that I would as a middle-aged person. But Generation Z has a bit more latitude, in my humble opinion, to say what is on their minds. Being respectfully vocal can be seen as confident, motivating, passionate, and engaging.

So, when I read their posts, I am incredibly proud that they have a desire to speak and of how they engage with others. They have learned when, where, and how to interact with the world around them. Are there times when I cringe at their posts, as the "old fogey?" Yes, and I sometimes will question such posts. But, ultimately, they have earned my trust. There were many bumps along the way, but we are on the other side of those now.

Hang tight, be diligent, and know you are protecting your children. That is the absolute best you can ever do for them.

SEVEN

BE A GOOD SPORT

(AND I'M NOT TALKING TO THE CHILDREN!)

We will use sports as an example to illustrate how we should approach our children's activities. Dance, music, art, or theater are also activities that can easily be interchanged with sports. They each require modeling the traits of "good sportsmanship" we would like our children to learn. While they differ in levels of competitiveness (or at least they should), they encompass participatory experiences that we all remember from childhood. So, sports are a good extra-familial activity to examine our parental responsibilities.

Parents seem to get their children involved in sports when they are very young. Children can begin playing soccer at 3. Three! I recall when mine were 3, they were starting to become more coordinated. Now, this does not mean that I resisted the trap of signing my children up for soccer at that ripe old age. And we did it for the same reason many others do: partly to get some exercise, partly to teach them about team sports etiquette, and partly (OK, more than "partly") for us to see our friends and socialize.

Our weekly schedule included practice sessions, their

Saturday games, and getting ice cream. Although these recreational activities are designed to be an introduction to sports, light-hearted, and fun for all, some, however, take youth sports a bit more seriously as if these games are being played at a professional level. In case you are wondering, please remember that there are rarely college or professional scouts at youth sporting events. There's no one to tell your child's coach that your child will be a multi-million-dollar athlete with brand endorsements. They can, though, enjoy sports throughout their life along with learning about camaraderie, team building skills, and the motivation to work hard.

Do not be offended by the previous paragraph. Your child may indeed become a professional athlete. Maybe they *are* a prodigy. Perhaps they have the talent and, with the right coaching, could become a professional athlete. Your child's ticket to financial freedom may indeed come from sports. You be you. No one is judging you or squelching your dreams. In fact, if your child is outstanding in their particular sport, contact me. I would love to follow their journey!

But most children participate in these sports for the pure enjoyment of playing. That is all. And guess what? It's OK. It's OK for them to enjoy something without being career-minded about it. There will be plenty of time to worry about their careers later. Sometimes, if we push too hard for them to be better, stronger, and more competitive, then the love and enjoyment subside, and children begin to resent that sport/activity.

When my children were young, I viewed myself as a calm, cool parent, at least in a sports setting. I saw myself as one who understood that my children were the ones playing, not me. I did not particularly appreciate watching crazy parents yell at their children from the bleachers. And I did not want to be the parent who yelled at the coaches for not making the right play call, screamed at other people's children for not making the right play, or snarked at other parents because their child made a mistake.

Unfortunately, many parents do behave this way. These parents put a tremendous amount of pressure on their children and everyone else, for that matter, and make it an unpleasant and uncomfortable place to be. We've all seen parents, whether in person or on video, yelling, screaming, and even fighting at games. And we all wonder, "Who on earth can lose their temper at a youth sporting event?" Get it together, people!

The Purpose

So, let's take a moment to share the purpose for putting our children in sports programs. As parents, we need to step back and have some perspective. Take time to soul-search and ask what we, as parents, are looking to gain from enrolling our children in youth sports activities:

- Are we simply looking for an activity for our children to participate in?
- Do we want them to learn social skills?
- Do we want them to learn how to work in a team setting?
- Will we push them to become professional athletes?
- Are we placing our children in that sport because we want to live vicariously through them?
- What about the fact that I am uber-competitive and want my child to be as well?

Regardless of where you fall on the spectrum described above, it is important to keep in mind that these sports must be about your child, their interests, and their talents.

Wait. What?! Yes, I hate to burst your bubble, but youth sports are about your child. They are learning how to play by rules, learning to be a team player, and learning how to follow through on their commitments—all things that will benefit them as teenagers and young adults. All these activities and the lessons associated with them teach lifelong skills that can be transferred to their schools, their careers, and their own families. Let's break some of these lessons down:

- When children learn the rules of a sport, they begin to learn how to follow directions and live within parameters. It helps them understand that we live in a world of rules that must be abided by to ensure everyone's safety and well-being.
- When children learn to play on a team, they begin to understand that they can accomplish more by working together. Playing a team sport means coming together as a group of people who support each other to achieve a common goal. This is one of the most critical life lessons learned in team sports. This skill is most helpful when our children begin working in a professional environment and must collaborate together with a team to complete their project or assignment.

Sidebar: My father coached my soccer team when I was in middle school. Soccer teams were co-ed in those days because there were not many girls playing at that time. Our team made it to the championship match where we were clearly the underdogs. One of the better players on our team failed to be a team player that day by "hogging" the ball because he wanted to be the MVP of the team. Dad was intolerant of his behavior and took him out of the game close to the end of the match due to his lack of sportsmanship. I still remember all the parents getting angry at my dad for doing this. After all, this was the championship match. A lot was riding on it. But Dad did not budge until the player apologized for his behavior and promised to engage his teammates on the field. Dad put him back on the field —just in time for him to score the match-winning goal and secure our win.

This sounds like a made-for-movie scenario, but it's exactly what happened.

This was a powerful lesson for that particular player and all the other players and parents on our team. Being a team player superseded the outcome of the match. This holds true in the workplace or anywhere else where two or more people are asked to complete a task. There is almost always a supportive team behind any successful person.

Following Through on Your Commitments

When children learn to follow through on their commitments, they understand the important lesson of not quitting. Many times, in a work environment, when working on a team or even on individual tasks, others are counting on you just as you are relying on them. In sports, if your child has committed to play on a team, they must follow through for at least that season, even if they are not enjoying it. The team is counting on your child to pull their weight. This is one of the most important life lessons we learn from group sports and one we should be teaching our children throughout their young lives.

Now, certainly there are times when it may be necessary to quit. A family emergency, a mental or physical issue arises, or some other pressing matter may make it necessary to leave the team. You, as the parent, are the best judge of each situation.

The Lessons We Need to Learn as Parents

In order to instill strong team-building skills in children, parents should also model appropriate behavior. At sporting events, it is important to realize that children learn by watching what we do. Children react to certain situations based on how their parents react.

That means we have to be adults. Sometimes that is easier said than done. Often, in the excitement of the game, emotions take over. It can be tough to control them when we become frustrated if a player or team is not living up to our expectations. But how do we model good sportsmanship when we are struggling to control our own emotions? Here are some strategies that may help you survive the soccer match when you find yourself frustrated:

- Bite your tongue if you cannot say anything nice.
- Take a quick walk around the bleachers, the field, or even the parking lot to calm down.
- Talk to the coach *after* the game to discuss your concerns (do not do it during the competition).
- Realize that you are not the one playing. Your child is. Before complaining, ask yourself if your child would be proud and supportive of what you are saying? Or are you embarrassing them?
- If you cannot control your outrage, then it is likely better for you to stay home. I know that is not what you want to do, but it may be best for your child.

Remember, this is NOT about you! Parents need to remember to model the behavior they want their children to learn. Children learn much more from observing behavior than from listening to you tell them how to behave. So, be the role model your child needs and deserves.

Competition Can Bring Out the Worst in People

Parents want their children to be successful. When our children are born and we hold them for the first time, we have so many hopes and dreams for them. We aspire for them to be more comfortable and successful in life than ourselves. We want to provide them with every need they could possibly have. We want them to find their passion, pursue it, and excel in it.

Bob Cook, a youth sports blogger, reminds us of that perspective in describing his own approach to watching his child play sports: "not caring does not mean that I have no desire to support my daughter and her team and see them do well. It does not mean I make a point of being actively hostile to the other parents. It just means that I am taking things, as the sports cliché goes, one game at a time".

Parents want to be supportive in whatever ways they are able.

But sometimes, when we take a normally calm rational person and place them in a competitive environment like a soccer match their child is playing in, they can become a completely different person—belligerent, incoherent, and short-tempered. They start yelling at their child, other players, and even the coaches. They turn into someone we would not recognize off the field.

I am fairly confident if we saw someone like this, we would not want to hang around them. And we certainly would not want our children to mimic their behavior.

So, as we head out the door with our children's cleats, juice boxes, and folding chairs in hand, think about how your behavior affects your children. What do you want them to learn from you? What do you want them to emulate? And how would you like to be perceived by others? In fact, I would go so far as to say that we, as parents, also have to prepare for "game day." Just like our children, we need to get our minds and attitudes in the right place—not in an effort to play the game, however, but in an effort to be the best supporter possible.

My hope and belief are that you want to be viewed as your child and team's cheerleader.

This is not to say that you cannot show your competitiveness. We all like to win and be successful. A few ways to be positive during competitions are:

- Speak in a positive tone when you are criticizing/cheering. Speaking in a non-threatening manner can be the difference between a contentious and a calm discussion, and even the outcome you desire from the situation.
- Role reversal. You would not take kindly if someone spoke ill of your child, so never, EVER, speak ill of another child. It does not matter whether that child is struggling to play; it is in everyone's best interest to stay quiet if you cannot be supportive.
- Praise your children and their teammates. Does it harm anyone if you tell another child, or adult for that matter, something positive they did? Even if it is the smallest flattering detail that you can share, share it. It will boost self-confidence and encourage them to work harder.

Punam's Perspective

The first thing you should know is that I am a fairly competitive person. I love the competition. And, of course, I love winning.

It never occurred to me how competitive I was until my oldest started playing soccer at the age of three. Unfortunately, I became the epitome of a soccer mom by taking her to her practices, watching her, and then giving her pointers on the way home. I am sure if she knew how to at that age, she would have rolled her eyes at me.

I soon realized that I needed some self-reflection or I was going to turn into "that parent." Realizing that this was about her having fun and learning, I had to step back and learn to yell inside my head. This was a part of my parent maturation process. I needed to understand my children were not going to be star soccer players, professional musicians, or ballerinas. In all honesty, that recognition was a tough one as I wanted to believe that my children were prodigies.

My kids were good at sports, don't get me wrong. They played hard, were competitive, and enjoyed their respective competitive activities, but they were not destined to become professional athletes. Since my children's talents were not going in this direction, we did what many families do—focused on education. By the way, there is competition there, too. There is some inherent desire among families to compete and share whose child is going to the "better" college.

Parents are judged by these absurd criteria. Traditionally, successful parents are seen as those whose children have attended Ivy League colleges and work for Fortune 500 companies. I have found that this trait cuts across cultures and geographic locales. It is a game of one-upmanship to see whose child is better educated and more successful. Of course, this is just as outrageous as expecting that all children playing youth sports will become professional athletes.

Interestingly, after a conversation with a dear friend of mine about our children and competition, she shared something that has stuck with me for almost 20 years. "Life is all about perspective." The first time she said this to me, I was young and dumb. This was just a feel-good statement, right? One to make me ponder and reflect. I took it with a grain of salt. But over the next several years, she kept saying it to me, and, eventually, it became part of my vernacular.

When that happened, it began to impact my life, and I was able to pull myself out of a stressful situation and look at it from an aerial view. My perspective changed the way I viewed those competitive and stressful times.

Of course, I want the best for my children. I want them all to be the star in their professions. But living life with perspective has helped me realize that my children are doing exactly what they are capable of doing at that moment. I needed to embrace this instead of being the soccer mom and pushing my children to the brink of misery.

There is a fine line between pushing your child and knowing when you have gone too far. Each child is different, and your approach with them should also be different. So, understand your boundaries and limitations, as well as your children's. Being the proverbial soccer mom will not always get you and your children where you want everyone to end up. Be mindful of that and model how you want your child to react and behave in competitive situations.

Remember, *Life is all about Perspective*. When we are able to step back and remember the true purpose of sports, then, finally, the dream we had when we first held our children, as infants, comes true.

EIGHT

YIKES! THE HOLIDAYS ARE ALMOST HERE!

The holidays bring about visions of fun, family, and fellowship. Our focus turns to a time of celebration and making memories. While the holidays can bring a lot of joy, they are also notoriously maddening because we tax our brains and bodies by multitasking more than usual—and therefore adding additional layers of stress. We tend to do this by wanting everything to be perfect. Every activity can be daunting, so we must balance how to find joy during the holidays with surviving the season in the healthiest way possible, both emotionally and physically.

The children are home from school or college. They are on a different sleep schedule (the nocturnal one). It almost seems that there is a 24-hour diner happening in your house. We go to sleep with the kitchen cleaned up only to find a sink full of dirty dishes the next morning. The laundry is never-ending. Well, at least this is what happens at my house. These daily tasks are exhausting on regular days, but during the holidays, they seem to triple in intensity. AND, if you have a job outside the home, you still have deadlines to meet, meetings to attend, and many professional tasks and obligations to complete before the end of the year.

We said it was the holidays, so you are also likely entertaining your friends and family, which means lots of prep work and trips to the grocery store. If you are the gift buyer for your home, this adds additional anxiety because you know you always want to buy the *perfect* gift.

Does this sound familiar?

The holiday season can be an exhausting time of year. But it doesn't have to be this way. I will share a pro tip from my husband, who is much wiser than me: Breathe. Take a few deep breaths, and while you are doing so, keep reading, and I will share a few more tips that we have learned along the way.

Breathe

As mentioned above, one of the most important things I would recommend is that you breathe. And I do not mean regular breaths. I mean deep breaths. This is probably the hardest thing to remember when we are anxious and stressed because it means we should stop what we are doing and focus on something that is not on our task list. But here is something to think about: all the tension we feel actually makes us less productive. So, the fact of the matter is when we take a short break to focus on intentional breathing, it can help you find your calm. We are helping ourselves to re-center which reduces stress and relaxes the body, according to Seppälä, Bradley, and Goldstein in their 2020 *Harvard Business Review* article.

In its simplicity, breathing allows you to refocus your energies and priorities to accomplish those necessary tasks and then permit yourself to have some latitude on tasks that can wait.

Lists

Lists are my lifeline. It is a sense of accomplishment to put a checkmark next to the completed tasks. And we all need to feel positive about our work. Making a list of all the activities, events, and tasks helps you stay organized. If you can work without lists, you are one of those amazing people and I am incredibly jealous. Kudos to you! Many of us, though, are tethered to our lists regardless of whether they help keep us grounded or create a feeling of accomplishment. They also allow the rest of the family to visualize what needs to be completed and *maybe* offer some help.

I would always make a list of the next day's schedule and share it with everyone at dinner the night before. By sharing the tasks, your children can step up and take a job or two off your plate. You can even delegate some tasks to engage them.

Additionally, plan your menus and then make your shopping list. This will help prevent last-minute scrambling to get missing ingredients. And, while you're at it, go ahead and add 15 minutes of "me time" to your list.

Who's In?

Everyone in the family can pitch in and do *something* to share in those last-minute chores to prepare for the holidays. Here are some ideas to consider:

- Can someone in your family go to the grocery store and pick up that last-minute spice you forgot?
- Can someone run the vacuum cleaner for you?
- Can someone help with laundry? For example, anyone tall enough to reach the buttons on the washing machine can do laundry with proper

instructions. If you are lucky, they will also fold it and put it away. Ahh . . . the perfect dream. For preschoolers, you can make laundry educational by asking them to match the socks. And, if you are super lucky, they will also fold it and put it away.

- Can someone set and clear the table for you?

These are small tasks that your family can help accomplish to make the holidays a bit less daunting. Involving your family not only makes your life a bit easier, but they learn how to be a part of the team.

Praise

People will forget what you said . . . forget what you did, but they will never forget how you made them feel.–Maya Angelou

For parents, praise is a small but incredibly powerful tool. Praising children and family members for helping, regardless of the task, is paramount. It is your key to keeping your sanity and peace while showing continued support and appreciation.

We all enjoy being praised and will continue to volunteer to help if we feel appreciated. Ensure that you take time to acknowledge your team, even if it is a pat on the back. Though they may complete the task differently than you would like, be appreciative that someone made your day a bit easier.

Remember: breathe. Take a couple of deep breaths in, a couple of deep breaths out, and remind yourself what the holidays are actually about—making joyous, unforgettable memories.

Prioritize

Some of us love to add items that could wait to our holiday to-do lists "just because" or even "I want to get this done as it's been bothering me," not because it *needs* to be completed during the busyness of the holiday season. Here are some questionable tasks that I have seen people tackle during the holidays: (*Disclaimer, I have been guilty of ALL of these!*)

- Does the pressure washing of your driveway need to get done right now?
- Do we need to re-landscape the entire yard?
- Do we need to have the inside of the house painted?
- Does the carpet need to be changed while preparing for the holidays?
- Does the pantry need to be cleaned out and reorganized, or can you still get to the box of macaroni in the back?

The answer is generally, "It can wait." You may *want* to accomplish these tasks before the holidays. Most, though, are not necessary to complete at that very moment and can wait until afterwards. Now, if you have poisonous mold growing on your driveway or your carpet has a large red wine stain from your last party, then maybe you will want to see to that. But for the most part, those extra "can-wait" tasks we put on our plate are not going to alter the spirit of our holiday.

Family time

During the holidays, we often forget to dedicate time to our families in our quest to have a perfect celebration. The busyness and the business of the holiday can easily cut into quality family time. One of the best pieces of advice I ever received was to carve out 30 to 60 minutes of family time each day. That does not include dinner time. This can seem impossible, but if you prioritize it, then it is more likely to happen. Some fun ideas to create memories with the family include:

- Game night
- Trivia night
- Movie night
- Art night
- Playing an outdoor game or walking

Quality time with our family is precious and fleeting. We should cherish time with our children whether they are still at home, in school, coming home from college, or even bringing their own families with them. Make sure your family is a priority.

Today is the day!

The day of celebration has arrived. Your relatives are coming over. You are navigating how to ensure everyone has a memorable time. All of your hard work and planning is coming to fruition. You are hoping you did not forget anything significant, but there is not much you can do about it at this point. You are up early to make sure everything goes smoothly without any last-minute hiccups.

The first item of business is to take a deep breath and pat yourself on the back for making it to today almost unscathed with your to-do list. Then, plow forward to make it enjoyable for all, especially you. Again, enlist your family, assign them age-appropriate tasks, and get going! Peeling potatoes, snapping beans, setting the table. Whatever the tasks are, be sure to delegate them. Children want to be helpful, so include them in the preparation. Today is the day to share and conquer.

Usually, at some point during the day, someone will ask, "Am I doing this the right way?" The real question they are asking is, "Is it to your satisfaction?" It took me a long time to realize that their way was just as good and, in some cases, better than my way. But they are looking for validation on a job well-done, and we should provide that positive feedback.

Meal-Time

When you sit down at the dinner table, make sure there is something at the table for everyone to eat. Everyone will be much happier if they have at least one of their favorite dishes to enjoy. Even if you have to make chicken nuggets for that fussy old uncle visiting, he will be thrilled that you thought about him. And you will be remembered for making your guests feel special. It never hurts to bank those brownie points!

Party Favors

Party favors or keepsakes for family members is a wonderful way for them to remember the event. What do you give as party favors when your guests can range from infants to grandparents? It can be challenging to find a suitable keepsake. You can, though, create some beautiful, personalized gifts made by your children at a minimal cost that everyone will enjoy.

- Allow your children to put their artistic skills to good use. Have them draw pictures and use them as place cards for each family member who is coming.
- Children love taking pictures, so ask them to make

a holiday photo collage. They can be the event photographer who put together a collage to email to the attendees after the event.

Punam's Perspective

Let me share a personal story about the holidays.

One year, when my children were in middle and high school, my husband took them Christmas-tree shopping and I chose not to go. Blasphemy, right? I was telling my friend this, and her response was, "Oh my goodness, you let your husband take your children Christmas-tree shopping? How can you trust them to pick the right tree?" I found this quite humorous. How much influence could I exert on the selection of a Christmas tree when I was outnumbered five to one?

This was not really about the Christmas tree. It was about my children. But, alas, according to my friend, I did the unthinkable. I *let* my husband take my children Christmas-tree shopping without me. I trusted my family and realized it did not matter whether the tree was too big, too fat, too skinny, or too tall. Whatever it was, it was going to be perfect regardless of whether I was there or not. I felt like Charlie Brown—I was going to love the tree anyway.

Once I explained that I trusted my children and husband, she asked me, "Are you also going to let them decorate it by themselves?"

The younger version of myself would have said, "Absolutely not!" But now that I am older and worn out (and wiser as well), my answer was, "Sure, why not?"

They enjoy taking out the ornaments they made during their classroom parties in elementary school. They reminisce, laugh, and share stories about their childhood. That is much more important than having the ornament placed correctly on the tree. The glass ornaments went high, so no one would get hurt when they were younger. But other than that, it was their tree. It was their memories. And they took incredible pride in the finished product.

My advice to you is to relax and enjoy the experiences of the holidays. It's OK. Everything does not have to be perfect. Admittedly, I am by nature a perfectionist and I like things done a certain way. It also makes me a beast to be around, and that's not good for anyone. So, over the years, I have learned to take deep breaths and allow others to have ownership over their own memory-making experiences.

The roles in our home have slowly begun to reverse as my children have gotten older, and now they enjoy finding recipes to cook and preparing for the holidays. They still love to decorate the house. My involvement has evolved into a managerial role while the children take care of most of the tasks.

Now I get to enjoy all aspects of the holiday with much less stress and anxiety (although I will admit I still have more than I should). I get to be around my children, who are excited to be a part of the team. That is what I encourage you to do. Build those memories. Build their competence. Boost their self-esteem. So, as they are growing older, they feel empowered to go out, help you run those errands, create those dishes, and make the best mac and cheese you will ever have. It is important not only for you from a stress-level perspective but also for you to believe in your children and trust them to accomplish those tasks that they are capable of.

Just breathe.

NINE

DISCRIMINATION AND DIVERSITY

Discrimination comes in all shapes and sizes. We can discriminate using age, gender, race, sexual orientation, or any other mundane characteristic as a criterion. You can discriminate for any inconsequential reason. But not all discriminations are equal, nor are they inherently wrong. For example, you may be a discriminating movie-goer. You may have a discriminating taste in fashion or wine. Essentially, discrimination is merely making judgements based on a predetermined set of criteria. Sometimes we even discriminate because of a preconceived notion and may not have a concrete answer as to why we're doing it. However, discriminating against each other based on external characteristics (skin color, religious faith, ethnicity, social status, etc.) reveals a dark side of our personal selves.

Why? Why do we judge other people based on some meaningless criteria? Why do we judge someone based on a singular characteristic? Intellectually, most of us know this is wrong.

These biases usually develop early in childhood. We develop views about others by observing what society says, the peer group we associate with, and the traditions and customs (ideologies) our parents instill in us. As we grow older, those biases become more ingrained and can potentially become more irrational.

Here is an absolutely absurd example of an irrational bias that I have. I love all vegetables. I could be a vegetarian if I had a wider variety of culinary skills. But there is one poor vegetable that I cannot eat, under any circumstances . . . eggplant. There is something in the slimy texture, the lack of flavor, and the taste that I cannot get past. According to reliable sources, my mom makes the best Indian-spiced mashed eggplant similar to baba ghanoush. Everyone besides me finds it delicious. My mom loves it and could eat it three times a day.

It seems like a silly thing really, but it reveals a bias. Every time eggplant shows up at the table, I know that I will have to pass. It is not the cook nor the preparation and it's nothing personal against the eggplant. I just immensely dislike it in all forms. I guess I learned it from my dad whose dislike for eggplant is legendary in our family.

I share this silly example with you not to make light of the seriousness of unjust discrimination, but instead to show that we all have innate biases that cloud our perception of the world. Of course, more importantly than any vegetable-biases are discriminations that are harmful to those who look, speak, act, or believe differently than us. Those beliefs can actually impact the daily life, productivity and social status of those in our communities. Let's take a closer look at some of these.

Discrimination Against People

We often make judgements based on frivolous criteria, sometimes even on one singular characteristic. Some of the biggest challenges our society has faced in the past few years center around discrimination against different genders, races, ethnici-

ties, and sexual orientations. So, let's break these into cate-
gories, and then, after you have some background and context,
we will discuss ways to talk to your children about this all-
important topic.

Before you chat with your children about discrimination,
the first thing you must do is to reflect on these topics and
acknowledge your own ideals and views.

In regard to your own biases, remember:

- We all have them.
- Sharing your preferences reveals your vulnerability
  and makes you more human and relatable to adults
  and children.
- It allows your children to understand that you have
  faults, are willing to acknowledge them, and are
  willing to have an honest, open conversation.

Diane Hughes, Ph.D. and Howard Stevenson, Ph.D. offer
sage advice as we ponder what this discussion will look like.
"Don't expect to have 'the talk' about discrimination. It
shouldn't be one conversation. Rather, let the discussion be
open and ongoing." In other words, it should be a consistent
and intentional dialogue, not a one-off monologue.

Color of Your Skin

I immensely dislike, more than anything else, anyone judging
others based on the color of their skin. Regardless of anyone's
skin color, using that characteristic as a judgmental criterion is
demeaning and dehumanizing. How does being Black, White,
or Brown define you as a person? Does it change who we inherently are? We are making assumptions about someone because
of the color of their skin.

This is NOT OK.

Many people I know are not the same skin color as me. Should I make assumptions about their character based on that? It's not uncommon to look at Indians and say (at least to themselves), "They must be a doctor, lawyer, or engineer." If you are guilty of this, it's OK. We get it; you are connecting a stereotype (about Indian professional choices) and making an assumption based on what we look like. Many people have been conditioned by society to think this way when you see an Indian.

But I'm here to tell you that I am none of those. I am a parent and a former educator. Blood makes me queasy, so I could never be a doctor. I am not strong in math, so being an engineer is out of the question. And there are too many loopholes for me to keep up with all the laws to be a lawyer. However, in fairness to how these stereotypes are perpetuated, my husband is an engineer, and my brother is a doctor—both of whom are Indian.

Along similar lines, we make judgements about people who are Black. Notice my words. *People who are Black.* They are people first.

We have been conditioned to think that we are different than those who are Black.

This demographic has been persecuted for centuries, had their lives and liberties taken from them, and yet they keep trying to overcome the barriers society has placed upon them. It is time to change this thought process, to cultivate relationships with people who look differently than us.

It is only then that you can have real, meaningful dialogue and begin to understand their plight. When we all work on this together, we make our communities stronger. In mid-June 2020, we fell back into what has become a cyclical issue. The horrific death of George Floyd, a man who was Black, sent the country back in the streets to protest racial injustice. In conversations with the older generation, I learned that protesters in 2020 were comprised of more racial diversity than those in the 1960s during the Civil Rights Movement. Maybe the pendulum will finally swing in the right direction of humanity —all humanity. Or paraphrasing Dr. Martin Luther King, Jr., perhaps the arc of the moral universe is beginning to bend towards justice.

But how do you talk to your children about discrimination? We will provide tips at the end of this chapter after covering a few more differentiated groups.

Women

Discrimination occurs with women, as well. Women have, for years, received less pay than their male counterparts. Currently, in 2020, women are paid $.81 for every dollar a man makes, according to www.pay.scale.com. Huh? So, women have to work longer/more than they already do to earn less than a man. Hmmm . . . Take a moment to let that sink in. They work harder to earn their place in the workforce, to prove themselves capable, and to earn the respect of their colleagues. Yet by many of the metrics society uses to express value, women are judged to be less worthy.

Women often have many spinning plates in the air between work demands, family needs, and trying to make everything look seamless. They are always on the go trying to ensure everything is the best it can be. It is an exhausting job that has few to no breaks, weekends off, or built-in vacations.

Sexual Orientation

Another highly discriminated group is the LGBTQ+ community. Since their sexual identities do not align with the "marriage is between a man and a woman" concept, people discriminate against them.

Although there has been no identified "gay gene," there is research that suggests that sexuality is based on many factors, including heredity, environment, and life experiences. In a 2019 segment on PBS.org, ". . . researchers found that sexuality is polygenic—meaning hundreds or even thousands of genes make tiny contributions to the trait . . . But polygenic traits can be strongly influenced by the environment, meaning there's no clear winner in this 'nature versus nurture' debate".

One path is not *better* than the other.

In simplistic terms, the male/female relationship is for procreation purposes to ensure the human species does not become extinct. But if you are looking for someone you are attracted to, it can be someone of *either* gender.

The LGBTQ+ community has become more visible and has grown in numbers over the past several decades. The simple reason for this is that society is incrementally becoming more accepting of this community. Slowly, these individuals are finding their voices and are beginning to gain equal rights and the benefits that their heterosexual counterparts have.

Progress

In sharing this information with you, it is important to remember we are all in different spaces when we speak about discrimination. Some see progress, some see how far we need to go, and some see it as idle chatter. Wherever you are on this spectrum, it is incumbent upon you to keep an open mind.

Educate yourself on the issues facing these communities. By understanding and listening to the other's challenges, and by being willing to engage with other voices, we can gain new perspectives, make these biases less burdensome, and can begin to take the necessary steps to break down barriers. We not only make our lives better, but we do so for those around us and society.

Progress will occur.

Now, Talking to Your Children

Above we discussed a few types of discrimination and how it directly impacts people's lives.

Now we need to talk to our children. How do we do this?

Here is a pretty simple thought: *Have an honest, open conversation with your children. Be straightforward, share your own biases, and acknowledge your views to them.*

It can be a tall order as it can be painful to talk about our biases and share them with our children. They will have questions. They will want to know how you developed your biases.

So, be ready!

Here are some ways to talk with your child about discrimination.

Talk to your children when everyone is relaxed.

- I know this may seem obvious, but there is something cathartic about talking to your children about such social injustices.
- Listen. This is a two-way conversation. We can learn from our children, who may have a different perspective than we do.

- Keep the dialogue open as it is vital for children to feel secure in sharing their views with you.

Age-appropriateness conversation

- When you are talking to your child, it is crucial to share the information at a level so they can understand.
- Speak to them in a vocabulary that is easy for them to comprehend.
- By using words outside of their grasp, you are likely to lose their interest and not be as impactful.

Be authentic

- We have to be true to who we are. By not doing so, we are lessening our self-worth.
- Children have a sixth sense and will see right through you when you are not authentic.

Be emotional

- Discrimination, bullying, and hate are all horrible characteristics in people. No denying that. But we all have preconceived notions about others. (Remember the eggplant?)
- It is OK for you to show your children how these behaviors affect(ed) you.
- For children to fully grasp these topics' depths, you must show your vulnerability and be emotional in your talk with them.

Be open-minded

- Our children have different experiences than ours and are exposed to vastly different ideas and opinions. They have 24-hour access to all types of information that we could never have imagined.
- Being open-minded, having honest talks, and looking at issues from different sides will help build confidence and trust in your relationship with your child.
- Your willingness to think outside the box will also allow your child to do the same. They will become open to others' points of view.

Talk to people who are discriminated against

- Ask them to share their challenges and then ... listen.
- Ask them to share ways to improve our biases and then ... listen.
- Ask them what you can do to make a difference in your community and then ... listen.
- Ask them how you can help your child be more inclusive and then ... listen.

Listen

- That is the only way we learn.
- That is the only way we grow.
- That is the only way we change our beliefs.
- That is the only way we decrease discrimination.

Diversity

As you can imagine, diversity and discrimination go hand in hand. If you are discriminatory and your goal is to become less so, you should be open to listening and speaking with different groups so you can understand the challenges people face.

According to Merriam-Webster, diversity means *the condition of having or being composed of differing elements*. This is the first definition. If you keep reading, it says *the inclusion of different types of people* (*such as people from different races or color*).

All of this is true. I argue, though, that diversity may present itself in the differences in age, religion, socioeconomic class, and yes, even color. However, when we talk about diversity, our minds immediately go to race. We need to also be aware of the breadth of diversity around us and work to be inclusive of all aspects of how the word can be defined.

So, when some community-wide committees or local-leadership groups form, diversity is often one of the criteria for determining its leadership team. There is usually a consensus that there should be diversity on a committee, meaning that committees and groups should be composed of those citizens who represent the diverse perspectives and experiences of the community. We must understand the motivation when we live in a majority white community that Black, Asian, or people of another race or ethnicity are highly sought after. However, diversity does not only mean skin color. It describes many groups of people with diverse cultures, socio-economic status, sexual orientation, and education, just to name a few.

Is seeking diverse representation "good enough?" Should we focus on selecting members who can do the task and then look for someone from a diverse background to fill that token spot? We should be careful lest we send the message that people of diverse communities cannot contribute to the committee/group in the same way as the majority. Unfortunately, this is where the diversity conversation stalls in many communities.

How do we change this in our children since it is important for our community's future?

Punam's Perspective

Our children, community, nation, and the world deserve better. We should be teaching our children that the world consists of many types of people. Some of whom we will agree with and some we will not, but our judgment should be on common interests and character, not on characteristics like skin color or any other external identifier. As I tell my children, "Judge someone based on their character, not *a* single characteristic."

As a person of color, who grew up in Georgia in the 70s, I have faced discrimination because of my skin color, the way I speak, and the food I eat. As far as skin color goes, we were neither Black nor White, and we did not fit in anywhere. For many of my classmates, they did not even realize there was a country called India. They thought all Indians were Native Americans.

Discrimination was prevalent in the town in which I was raised. When I became an adult, I began to understand that we were often considered the "diversity factor." We fit the bill of being thoughtful, politically correct, and friendly, along with checking the box of being diverse (translation: brown-skinned).

Now, I want to believe in my heart, as I am an idealistic person, that many of those committees asked me to join because I brought a different perspective to the table. But I am also certain that I just checked the diversity box on some committees. Although checking that box may have been the initial reason, hopefully, over time, my ideas and contributions became more important than my skin color.

Is it hurtful? Yes. Is it demeaning? Yes.

It also means that we must continue to put one foot in front of the other, show others that we belong, are intellectually capable, and deserve to have a seat at the table and bring our ideas to the group.

Let us sincerely focus on understanding diversity and how to achieve it authentically, so there are no negative connotations associated with it. Let us make sure we start with ourselves, then model the behavior for our children. When we talk to our children, we need to be cautious with our words, thoughtful of their meaning, and open to hearing otherwise. Our children, and their friends who may not be the same color as them, deserve that. For everyone's sake.

TEN

A WHOLE NEW WORLD

It takes a village to raise a child.
—an African proverb

You have often heard that parenting is the hardest job you'll ever have. And you are likely reminded of this every day. When those days are challenging, you may need to enlist the support of your team: your significant other, your parents, your friends, and/or your village. But what happens when you choose to leave your village for a new one? One that is in another country that is culturally different than the one you know.

Everyone, and I mean everyone, is an immigrant in America. Unless you are Native American, your ancestors all came from a different land. Some arrived recently, while others have been here for generations. But at the end of the day, we are all from somewhere else.

The first formal immigrants to America were European. They came to an unknown land and had to figure out how to survive, build a community, create social networks, worry about food, clothing, shelter, and find a livelihood for themselves and their families. These are not new issues for immigrants. This is just one example from millions of foreigners who have settled in a country other than their own.

Why did the settlers come here? Why did they choose to leave the comfort of their country and homes to live in a place that would be vastly different?

They came to the New World to build a new life and to fulfill their dreams. To pursue what we call the American Dream.

This is the Dream stated in the Declaration of Independence that says "all men are created equal." As time has passed, more and more immigrants have come to this country from all walks of life, for all kinds of reasons, and from all kinds of places. Jobs, education, family, and health-related issues are just a few of the reasons for which people immigrate to America or any other country. Those who immigrate want to create a better life for themselves and their families. This bears repeating: *Immigrants settle in other countries to create a better life for themselves and their families.* This is so important because people everywhere are generally looking for a better quality of life. If they believe a new country can provide that, then they immigrate.

I can say this with some degree of certainty as my parents moved to America for better educational opportunities and an improved standard of living. Having been here for more than half a century, they have settled here and built a life for our family.

It was not an easy task as America is culturally quite unlike India. Almost everything is different. Arguably, one of the most unexpected and challenging parts of immigrating is figuring out the education system. The classroom environment, the presentation of material, and the subject content are just a few of the differences between the Indian and American education systems. Since I am most familiar with these two education systems, I will use them as the basis of comparison for the rest of this chapter.

America's Education System

In America, education is seen as a federal and state mandate. Much of what students learn stems from the government's guidelines, and teachers must teach to those standards. Teachers work incredibly long hours to manage various aspects of educating a child. These educational tasks include things such as direct instruction, mentoring, and being a confidante in certain situations.

Often, teachers face students who may have personal issues that inhibit their ability to focus in class. Their home life may have stressors. There may be some trauma that has occurred in their lives that prevents them from concentrating. There may be some learning disability that hinders their comprehension in a typical classroom environment. All of these can be factors teachers face when they enter the classroom each day.

In stark contrast to the Indian education system, which we will discuss next, students in America are given intermittent assessments throughout the year to determine progress. For example, teachers routinely give quizzes, chapter or unit tests, essays, or use some similar evaluation tool to determine a student's comprehension and mastery level. At the middle and high school level, a final exam or End of Year (EOY) exam may be given. Periodic testing allows teachers to understand their students' comprehension of the subjects and adjust their lessons accordingly.

For those students with special needs, there are provisions in place to ensure every child is educated to the best of their capabilities. Students who have mild challenges, such as dyslexia, may be included in a regular class with a special education teacher assisting or with accommodations to promote success. Students needing more individualized assistance are placed in a self-contained class where there is a lower student/teacher ratio to address their academic needs. And, in recent times, inclusion classrooms have become more standard: rooms in which students with special needs are combined with traditional students—all in an effort to provide all students with a free and appropriate education.

India's Education System

India's family, social, and educational systems are a hierarchical system where adults offer guidance and their decisions are highly esteemed. A child in this environment needs to focus only on their schoolwork. With that in mind, teachers in India are considered gurus. *Guru,* in Sanskrit, means spiritual leader, teacher, or expert. Teachers are revered without question as they are deemed all-knowing. They are trusted to teach their subjects independently. So, when children go to school, they must follow the teacher's instructions.

Not only do the students listen to their teacher, but so do their parents. Parents put all their trust in the teacher, they respect the knowledge they impart, and they heed the guidance they provide. It is exceedingly rare for an Indian parent to ever challenge the authority or competency of an Indian teacher. Of course, this has more to do with the Indian cultural milieu than any particular educational belief.

Another contrasting aspect of the Indian education system is that students take only one exam a year, much like an EOY exam that determines whether they will be promoted to the next grade level. There are no quizzes or chapter tests throughout the school year to assess mastery of a skill. This may sound exciting for those of you who have endured the stress of studying for weekly chapter tests or writing research papers with complex citations. You may think, "No tests throughout the course? Sign-me up!"

But this is incredibly stressful for those who see the benefits of periodic assessments for comprehension and mastery. In India, that one test assesses how much knowledge students have attained that year. If a student does not make passing marks, they will not be promoted to the next grade and will not be considered for future esteemed educational opportunities. Unfortunately, it will also probably affect their choice of colleges.

As you can imagine, this is a pressure-cooker situation for children and their families, and students take extra coaching classes and study continuously for months. Students pour themselves into studying for this ultimate test while their parents work to provide the necessary support their child needs to succeed. Parents take pride in sharing their child's scores. It is the indicator of an academically successful child and the result of good, focused parenting. It is fair, however, to question whether in this instance parents are focusing on the real value of education. Is it mastery/comprehension of a subject or is it a score on one test that we should be celebrating?

You might be wondering how the Indian education system handles those with special needs. Federal laws are in place that grant education for all children from ages 6-14. The Indian system is quite similar to the American education system in this manner. Those children who have mild disabilities and are able to be successful in a regular education classroom, are placed as such. Those who require more individualized education due to their disability are placed in a self-contained classroom with fewer children to receive the attention they need. Unlike America, though, there are no federal laws (Americans with

Disabilities Act) to ensure all buildings are accessible to all citizens yet, so, not all schools are equipped with ramps and elevators to accommodate those with physical disabilities. Therefore, the latter group, receives their education in a separate building.

Immigrants and Education

This is a true story, but I have changed the names to protect those involved.

Now that we have set the stage let's talk about a family, the Shahs, who immigrated to America in the 1970s.

The Shahs are parents to one son, Anup, who is eight years old. They left their small town in North India for the all-American, Midwest city of Chicago so Mr. Shah could pursue a professional opportunity. They will be here for at least the next five years.

They brought everything they could stuff into their suitcases (bed linens, pictures, and memorabilia) to make their new home feel cozy and comfortable. They arrive in June so they can adjust and prepare for the new school year. They buy a used car, learn how to buy groceries, and begin to build a social network. What they do not change, however, is how they communicate and eat. They still speak Hindi, their native language, and continue to eat their Indian comfort food of rice and lentils. It is their small way of staying connected to their heritage.

The Shahs begin settling into their new environment and getting Anup ready for the school year, where he will be in third grade. Once Anup has registered at the neighborhood public school, he receives an unusual (at least to them) school supply list. The Shahs have never had a school supply list that includes cleaning and teacher supplies. In India, schools provide those. The parent's only responsibility is to provide the daily items that children would use, like pencils, pens, and paper.

This is a whole new world for them. One the Shahs could not have imagined. Buying chalk, hand sanitizer, and paper goods are beyond what they thought they would need to buy for Anup to attend school. They will soon realize, though, that this is the tip of the iceberg of what they need to learn about this new education system.

During the first week of third grade, Anup learns that he will have spelling tests every Friday. He is wondering, "Every week? That's a lot of testing for only one subject. How many tests is the teacher going to give?" It was a foreign concept for him to be tested every Friday on ten spelling words. This seemed extreme to Anup and his parents. But remember, they are an Indian family, so they are conditioned not to question the teacher's methodologies.

Slowly, Anup begins to adjust to this new system. He feels like he is constantly studying to make sure he is ready for the next quiz or test. He is exhausted, but acclimating, and is excelling in his classes. His teacher is quite impressed with his performance. In the spring of the school year, Anup's teacher requests he be tested for the Gifted Program and sends a letter home asking his parents' permission for testing.

When Anup brings the letter home for his parents to sign, they sign it even though they are unsure about the program's purpose. In India, there are no gifted classes. Mr. and Mrs. Shah begin researching what they need to know about the Gifted Program and how it will help Anup. They decide that the Gifted Program will be a good fit for him with its enhanced hands-on experiences and more in-depth learning opportunities, so they grant permission for him to be tested.

Like many aspects of the education system, these assessments can take months to administer once the paperwork is signed. A month has passed, and the Shahs are getting anxious because the evaluation has not been administered. But they are asked to wait patiently. And so patiently, they wait. Finally, the day arrives, and Anup takes the initial assessment to see whether he meets the program's initial qualifications. Then, more waiting.

When the results come back weeks later, Anup learns he did not attain the necessary score to be admitted into the Gifted Program. He is devastated. His parents try to console him, but there is no use. They tell him he is still smart, and that one test does not define him though in their hearts, they fear it actually might. Anup still feels like a failure. He knew all the other students would look at him differently. Even more different than they already did.

Anup's academic confidence is shattered. His effort and grades begin to drop immediately. He becomes a mediocre student who no longer cares about his education.

His parents continue to build Anup's shattered spirit. They come from a culture where you never questioned teachers and administrators. When the test results came back, they did not know that they could ask the teacher for other options, including alternative ways to be tested. They did not know that there is a policy in many school districts to have your child retested at the school in one calendar year or even privately tested.

Anup's mediocrity follows him through middle school, high school, and college. He manages to squeeze by in his studies and get average grades. But his passion for learning had all but faded until college, when his Hinduism professor ignited the spark that was silenced for so long. The professor connects Anup with his heritage, with his religion, with his inner being.

Suddenly, his passion comes alive again, and he becomes a sponge wanting to absorb whatever he can. He is so excited to wake up and go to class, something he has not felt in more than ten years. He feels like he is making up for the lost time. After finally settling on a degree in economics and graduating with honors, he ultimately becomes a successful CEO of a large, multinational financial company.

The Moral of the Story

The Shahs' story is not an unusual one, in fact, it is a common one for most working-class immigrants. Being an immigrant is a tough haul.

Perhaps if the teacher knew the Shah family was new to the country and did not understand the nuances of the education system, their experiences would have been less traumatic. Although the chips fell this way for Anup, he was still able to create his own success story out of his adversity. Unfortunately, not every immigrant student is so fortunate.

What You Need to Know

Mary Tamer, in her 2014 article, offers an insightful assessment of immigrants and their encounters with the United States' education system(s):

Even though one out of every four children in the United States is an immigrant or the U.S.-born child of immigrants, many schools are ill-equipped to meet their needs. Immigrant youth frequently are learning two languages, an incredible asset, but one that many schools have yet to learn to support effectively. Using multiple forms of communication in the classroom and supporting native language development takes skill and practice. The demands of standardized testing often force schools instead to emphasize rote learning in English, neglecting the incredible asset of children's native languages and much of what researchers have discovered about how children learn second languages.

Regardless of how long you have lived in America or any other country you choose to immigrate to, there is an adjustment or acclimation period. All immigrants eventually begin the process of assimilating and adjusting culturally. While some cultures may require the "home culture" be maintained at home, they almost always expect family members—especially children—to start learning the nuances of the adopted country's culture and norms. This process comes into stark relief when immigrant families must deal with the highly bureaucratized and hierarchal systems such as social service agencies and, of course, the education system.

Anup's journey is typical for children who are coming from other countries. Many children struggle in school when English is not their first language. It can be detrimental to their confidence and ability to test (as in Anup's case), especially on a culturally-biased assessment. Cultural bias in testing refers to a test that is not assessing a student's knowledge on the subject and uses information that the student may not have experienced in their lives due to their social environment.

The Shahs faced challenges as they were not privy to ins and outs of the American education system, and they learned the hard way that they could question and even challenge the bureaucratic systems in place. Although the Shahs did not force a change for Anup, they were quite vocal with their immigrant friends. By sharing Anup's story, they ensured their friends' children were given those opportunities that Anup had missed.

We often make mistakes raising our children. That is how we learn what we should and should not be doing. Through our mistakes, we can also teach others. It is probably one of the main reasons moms commiserate about raising children—to learn from each other. When you are from another country, though, the challenges are magnified because:

- You do not know the new country and its nuances.
- You are behind the "cultural knowledge" curve about the country.
- You are not quite sure how to navigate the education system due to a lack of experience.
- You likely will be too timid to contact the school or principal and instead tend to gravitate to those from your native land who are probably facing the same challenges you are.
- You are counting on those in the education system to guide your child.

Punam's Perspective

The Shah's story is personal. I know the "Shah" family. They are very close friends of ours. Yet, they are similar to thousands of others who have decided to make America their home. As a child of immigrant parents, I would like to share some of my thoughts with you regarding what you can do to help them.

First, make an effort to empathize with the challenges these parents encounter. You can do this by getting to know them on a personal level. Talk to them. Their desire for their children is no different from yours—to have their child be as successful as possible. It is what we all strive for.

Second, try and understand that their initial learning curve may be steeper than yours as there is so much to learn about this new land. New immigrants are learning the systems in the country with which you are already familiar.

And finally, for one moment, put yourself in their shoes. Imagine being in an unfamiliar country, where you are choosing to create a new life for your family. But there is a cost associated with that decision—having to learn how the country works and being away from your support system. Wouldn't you want someone to extend a helping hand to you? Someone to answer those difficult questions and give you a head's up on how to navigate the education system?

The dream to excel lives within every citizen and every immigrant. When we work together, we can create a more productive, cohesive world for everyone.

ELEVEN
PARENTING THROUGH A PANDEMIC

This chapter is based on a live edu-Nar (webinar) offered by edu-Me in Spring 2020 while we were all quarantined in our homes during the COVID-19 pandemic.

We have all been stuck at home, right? It's crazy. We've been together for several weeks and are probably ready to get back into the real world in some way, shape, or form. Whether you are already back to work or still cooped up inside the house, there has been a huge, sudden shift in how parents and children approach their daily responsibilities since the country shut down due to this pandemic. And now we are semi-open and hoping that the worst is over.

In the meantime, we need to figure out how we will manage all the tasks on our plate.

Barbara DeBaryshe, Director of University of Hawaii's Center on the Family asks parents to be aware of how stress affects their child, especially during this time. "Your child's behavior is not misbehavior, it's a signal. It's communication of their fears, feelings of loss, or confusion. So as much as you can, stop and think about your child's perspective," she explained.

I held an edu-Nar (webinar) where parents had a chance to ask their pressing questions regarding how to navigate this unconventional time. Below are some of the questions and the discussions that followed.

Q: My husband and I are both working from home. Our hyperactive children are with us too, since schools are now closed. How can I manage it all?

A: We will discuss the hyperactivity part in a bit. But here is something to keep in mind: we are ALL in the same boat. The age of the children does not matter in this situation. We've all been inside the house or, at the very least, in the same space, with limited activities and social interaction other than with those cooped up with us. Generally, this is an excellent recipe for a child or parent "time bomb."

Having a schedule for the entire family helps with the expectations of when you are available to play, assist with homework, or answer questions. For young children, it is advantageous to use a timer for certain activities. This way, there is an audible indicator when one activity ends, and the next begins. For example, if you have a conference call from 9 a.m. to 10 a.m. and you need the children to stay quiet, use a timer for that block of time and let them know you are unavailable until they hear the "ding." You wouldn't do this for children who can tell time, but this method does allow you to carve out specific times for those important tasks where you cannot be interrupted.

You can also teach them that your work is a priority during

specific parts of the day and let them know when you are available to have some quality time with them.

Now, let us discuss the hyperactivity piece.

It can be challenging to have children jumping all over the place while you are trying to work. You have to figure out how to deal with all that pent-up energy while taking care of the responsibilities of your job and keeping up with your household duties. Hyperactive children need more structure. So, creating a specific, workable schedule for them is imperative. The activities cannot be too long, or they will lose focus and start wandering, both physically and mentally.

The biggest thing I found with my children, especially when they were younger and wanted to run around and do everything with me, was to create a schedule. We had a block of time for different activities. If your child can finish only five math problems before needing a break, then take a 5-minute break by letting them stretch or some other short activity before working on the next set of problems.

You should also carve out 45 minutes of free time a day—equivalent to recess. Letting them run around and have your undivided time allows them to feel secure and loved. And you are spending quality time with them. Think of fun activities you can do together during those 45 minutes, like playing tag, frisbee, or a musical instrument.

Afterward, though, everyone goes back to work.

Since we are not in a brick-and-mortar school right now, we, as the teacher, can allow this more flexible, independent learning to occur. Although this may not be the ideal situation where you can block out specific times to get *your* work done, building in that flexibility may help everyone be more productive.

. . .

Q: We are currently homeschooling our children because schools are closed. How can we ensure our child doesn't get behind academically?

A: First of all, there is a distinct difference between home-schooling and schooling from home. Homeschooling means that parents or guardians are the teachers. They are researching and creating the curriculum taught to their children. Most of us are schooling from home. This means that our children, in non-pandemic times, attend school in a physical building for a part of the day and are taught by certified teachers. Right now, if you are schooling from home, you are helping them with assignments provided virtually by their teachers.

By the way, neither is easy. Both require work to make sure your child is completing their assignments, comprehending the material, and showing some level of mastery. When schooling from home, though, you are in an "On the Job Training" (OJT) situation. You are quite literally learning on the job how to teach your child. This can be daunting and overwhelming especially if teaching does not come naturally to you and you are worried your child will be academically behind when they head back to their traditional learning environments.

But, alas, do not worry. There is help! Lots of it. There are resources galore for you and your child. First, start with your child's teacher. The teacher is the one person your child is accountable to in terms of grades and promotion. They also happen to know your child, so there is a personal investment in their academic success. Reach out to them and ask for advice and, hopefully, they will be able to guide you.

Another great resource is online tutoring. You can Google just about any question, and there is someone who has uploaded a tutorial. Go ahead and search for "how to conjugate verbs." There are hundreds of videos for your child to learn from. You can also look for a one-on-one tutor who can work specifically with your child.

A note of caution: Monitor what your child is searching for on the web and make sure they are on reputable sites. Your child's safety is of utmost importance.

Q: Help! I have too much on my plate and cannot find time to get everything done. What can I do?

A: Some parents look like they have it all together. You know the type. Always smiling, calm, and can seemingly do everything successfully without flinching. How on earth do they balance it all and make it look so easy? I hate to burst your bubble, but they probably are struggling just like you. Some may have it all together, but I'm speaking to the rest of the 99.9% of us. Most of us are lucky we could get the kids up, fed, and dressed— without anyone having a major meltdown.

We all have the same number of hours in the day. We have to choose what is necessary for that day and what will have to wait. Prioritizing your tasks for the day helps you stay organized and keeps your stress levels down. Some days you will feel you are on top of the world since you checked off everything on your list and maybe even completed a few additional tasks. Other days will be frustrating because you haven't checked as many boxes for the day as you would like. There are days where your children need a bit more attention to get them to complete their homework or some other task. It is OK to spend that time to help them if nothing is pressing that you are needed for at that moment, like a professional deadline.

Think about it this way: If your child will become frustrated or have a meltdown because of the task, it is better to spend that time on the front end with them to help. Otherwise, the outcome can require more time and become more frustrating on the back end.

The most prominent theme here is to be patient with everyone around you, especially with yourself. Remember, there are only 24 hours in the day. Here are the most important things to remember that we MUST do in a day for our children:

- Children must be fed.
- Children must be clothed.
- Children must be loved.
- Children must feel safe.

Not rocket-science things, but at the end of the day, children need these things. Everything else is a bonus! It's important to remember this and realize we are not going to get everything done, so be patient and complete those tasks that are within your control and your schedule.

Q: I have a reasonably independent middle-schooler. While she is schooling from home, how much should I monitor her e-learning?

A: Middle and high-school students are in a transitional phase in their lives. They are facing physical and emotional changes. They are also asserting their independence and trying to figure out their place in the world. Not to mention their academics are also becoming more intense. This is a challenging time for almost every child in some capacity.

This can be true for parents as well. We are not exactly sure how hands-on we need to be. Should I hover over them? Should I let them try on their own and then swoop in when they can't figure it out? Should I let them do it entirely on their own and hope for the best? E-learning is new to most of us. Many of us did not grow up with computers. I know it may be hard to believe, but I did not have a cell phone until I was almost thirty! But I digress. Our children have never known a world without computers and cell phones. Their ability to complete assignments and attend virtual classrooms is much easier than for those of us who did not grow up with technology.

Even as an independent learner, they still may want or need you to check their work to make sure they have understood the concept correctly. Since you are also working while they are studying, it may be prudent to check in with them when it is convenient for you both. This way, all of your work tasks are complete, and they have had a chance to complete their assignments as much as they can independently.

If your child needs more hands-on attention, you must carve out time in the day to address their questions when you can focus solely on them, uninterrupted. Now, if you struggle with a particular subject, then you will need to find someone to help them. Tutors can be lifesavers. Tutors can be anyone who can help your child understand a concept in a particular subject. They can be teachers, friends, a mentor, a private tutor, or even someone online. All of these are options for you to employ to ensure success.

Keep in mind it is your responsibility to take the initiative and find that person, especially if the child is younger. By doing so, you are showing your child that you are prioritizing their education.

. . .

Q: *How can you keep high-school children, especially seniors, motivated when they are schooling from home?*

A: It is difficult when life takes an unexpected turn and our regular, pre-scheduled days are turned upside down—especially when keeping yourself and your child motivated can be tough even on an average day.

When life changes, motivating children can be extra challenging. They are out of their routines and may not see the value in completing their assignments. But you understand how important that is, so you have your work cut out for you, especially if you have a senior.

So, what can you do? Here's the scoop: lots of our children's time at school is taken up with non-academic, bureaucratic stuff: attendance, switching classes, lunch, calling roll, etc. The actual academic teaching time is shorter, about 3-4 hours a day in high school. If your child is struggling to keep to the school schedule, no worries. They only need just a few hours a day if they are efficient with their time. That said, it can still be frustrating when children are not motivated to study, even for that decreased amount of time. The goal is to figure out what motivates them and use it as a reward. For example, if you have a job, you get paid (a reward) for your work. If you cook, your bonus is to eat what you have made.

Incentivize them to finish their schoolwork by letting them play a game on their Nintendo Switch, bake their favorite dessert, or spend the afternoon reading a book once they have completed their assignments. The goal for *you* is to get them to finish their schoolwork.

· · ·

Q: How can we prioritize our children's physical and mental health while they are committed to a school schedule?

A: Traditional school days can be a time-zapper. Whether children are homeschooled or schooled at home, the assignments, projects, and tests can throw you into a tailspin between teaching your children and the other demands on your time with seemingly little to spare for anything else. Your child's health can become a secondary or tertiary issue for you to think about. However, now that many children are at home, it also becomes necessary to keep them physically moving at some level.

Exercise must be scheduled like all other critical items, such as meetings, tests, study sessions, and meals. If you prioritize it, it will get done. That is the first hurdle.

The second is: What kind of exercise will they do? Running? Obstacle courses? Tennis? Weights? Online exercise classes?

In the summertime, it is easy to be outdoors and be active. Wintertime is a bit more challenging for many because it can be too cold to be outdoors. Indoor exercise may not be as exciting for some but including it in your daily routine will help everyone become physically and mentally stronger.

There is no shortage of exercise options. Parents should provide opportunities that are safe and age-appropriate for children. You will also have more buy-in if you participate with them. Children want to model what you do, so model an exercise routine that works for you. They will follow. Once they see how important it is to you, they will incorporate it into their schedules and, hopefully, carry it throughout their entire lives.

After all, our ultimate goal is that we want our children to become independent, healthy people.

Punam's Perspective

Parenting is like trying to play darts with a moving board. Each day is different. You never know what you are going to get with varying levels of exhaustion, workload, and emotions. Our job is to assess the situation and immediately troubleshoot any issues that arise, not only at home with our children but also at work. Children may not be able to express it appropriately and consistently to you, but their challenges are similar to ours.

While teaching them at home can be difficult, we must also remember to provide physical and mental support as much as possible.

One day, when she was in middle school, my oldest daughter asked when her dad was going to be home.

"Later," I said.

"Well, I need help with geometry. I don't understand this concept," was her response.

"Maybe I can help." After all, I had taken the class some 25 years earlier. Surely, I could retrieve some information (note sarcasm)!

"I don't think so; it's math."

"OK, well, can I look at it to see if I may know how to help?"

Reluctantly, she showed me the problem, assuming that I would never know the answer because I was now a stay-at-home mom, and her dad was the engineer. And after dusting off the cobwebs of the geometry file in my brain and going through a bit of relearning, I was able to deduce how to help her solve the problem. She was surprised and, hopefully, a bit proud.

I wore my SuperMom cape happily that day. However, the lesson for both of us was not to underestimate what the other knows. It elevated the level of respect we have for each other simply by connecting on a topic outside our normal ones.

We all have challenges that occur in our lives, no matter who is the adult and who is the child. Whether it is meeting a deadline, studying for a test, or trying to motivate ourselves to complete another project, we need encouragement and support. By carving out some time to help your child with their homework, discuss an issue that is upsetting them, or giving them a pat on the back for a job well done, you will create a positive, supportive, and secure environment so when challenges do arise, there is a trust factor built into the relationship to support each other.

TWELVE
EMPTY NESTING

It's hard to imagine when you are holding your newborn that there will be a day when your child will grow up and become an independent adult. That the 18 or so years will fly by, and you will end up an empty-nester.

When my oldest was born, I held her and looked at my parents, asking them, "I am supposed to take care of her only for the next 18 years?" Although I knew inherently that I could raise her to be a kind, compassionate, productive citizen, I think my real question was, "What happens when she leaves and goes off to college?" That question preoccupied and, quite frankly, scared me for her entire childhood. In the back of my mind, I knew she would grow up and head out to start a life of her own.

I know I am not the only parent who feels this way. But what can we do to prepare for the day when we say, "See ya later!" to the little beings we have raised, and they are now leaving the nest?

Having an empty nest is an emotionally-charged period in our lives on so many levels. It is the question I was asking my parents when my oldest was a newborn. It is the fear of the unknown and the nervousness of the risks of letting her fly solo. And it all came to fruition in the blink of an eye.

You feel that you have not spent enough time with them. You are wondering if you have given them the skills they need to be independent. You hope you have instilled a sense of values and a spirit of confidence that will allow them to lead to a positive, fulfilling life.

Thinking about these challenges can make you crazy. But, in reality, you have to trust that you are giving them all the tools they need to succeed. And if children know they have your emotional support when needed, they will reach out to you when they have a question or concern.

Prepare Yourself

Who am I kidding, there is no real way to prepare yourself for the emptiness you will feel when your child leaves home on a permanent basis. As hard as you try, the sudden life changes you encounter when you pass by their vacant bedroom, sit at the dining room table and see their empty chair, and miss those lively discussions are all signs of the void your child leaves behind.

We can, though, be intentional and focused on how to best spend our days so that they are beneficial and meaningful. This may not be easy, but when we reflect on what we can do, we can accomplish more and feel more content.

Max D. Gray suggests that "You should think about those things that contribute to your well-being. The relationship between parents and children often improves when they are no longer at home. Another aspect is the time with which you now have to devote to new projects".

So, here are a few ideas that may help you with this

transition.

- Talk to other parents who have become empty nesters. They may have an insight into how they coped with their own children's leaving that may be beneficial for you.
- Find a new hobby that you can dive into once the house is empty. You may begin playing a musical instrument, a new sport, reading, or writing projects.
- Share your apprehension with your significant other or a trusted confidante.
- Take a deep breath and realize this is the new normal. Even though you may not want to believe it, sending your child into the world is a natural progression for them to become independent.
- Pat yourself on the back for having done an excellent job. Raising a child is no joke, and we often focus on the things we have not done well. Now is the time we should remember that we have raised a remarkable child. And our role as our child's parent/teacher continues even though they may not be physically living at home.

Prepare Your Child

Your child is likely ready to spread their wings and have some independence before you are quite ready for it—if you can ever really be ready. They are prepared to conquer the world and honestly believe they are invincible. They no longer have a curfew or have to check in with you before making their plans.

Before they head out the door, though, some ground rules need to be set. Even though they are not technically under your roof, there are some basic rules they need to understand that will keep them as safe and protected as possible.

- Let them know what is important to you.
- Let them know you love them and are proud of them and cannot wait to see them fly.
- Let them know you are a phone call away from helping them through a situation.
- Let them know that they will make mistakes, but it is vital for them to learn from them.
- Let them know how you feel about their exposure to alcohol and drugs.
- Let them know there are personal, societal, and potentially professional ramifications and physical dangers of specific actions like drinking and driving or smoking pot. Actions we know our young adults are exposed to.

Anecdote:

When my husband and I took each of our children to college, we implemented all the tips given above. The last one was the most serious of the discussions we had with them. We were not naïve enough to think our children were not going to drink before they turned 21. In fact, we were sure they would. It is just what children do at that age.

But there were some ground rules that we shared with them to think about before they drank to ensure they stayed safe.

As young people, they can feel that they are indestructible and can overcome anything. That societal rules do not apply to them. So, if they chose to drink, the rule for our children was that they were not to drive or get into a car with anyone in their group that had more than one drink.

Also, they should drink only with people they knew and

trusted. Those who will take care of them if they need help. I am
a bit old-fashioned, so this was more for my girls than my boys.

Now, I am using drinking as an example, but it can be interchanged with anything you deem worthy. Drugs, joining Greek life, or even academics.

The point here is that you need to arm your children with the tools they need to make well-informed, mature decisions to have fun but understand the consequences of excessive behavior.

What Happens When They Actually Leave?

When you drop your child off for the first time and get them settled into their new surroundings, it is exciting, terrifying, and sad all at the same time. You are proud of their accomplishments so far and look forward to what the next chapter of their lives will bring. You are looking forward to watching them mature into productive citizens.

But what happens to you? From the day they were born, you have poured your heart and soul into raising your child. Each day you woke up and vowed to do your absolute best to provide everything you could for them. Made sure they completed their homework, sent follow-up emails to their teachers, took them to their extracurricular activities, held birthday parties, and much more.

You have worried about their academic success, socioemotional development, and reasoning skills, to name a few. Now, you are dropping a piece of your heart off and leaving them. Some of you will likely go through some of the five stages of grief:

Denial: My child is just at a sleepover party and will be back in the morning.

Anger: Why has my child left me after all I have done for

them? How can they just get up and leave me?

Bargaining: I promise to carve out more quality time with my child if they come back home.

Depression: I am sad that I was not as present as I should have been during their childhood. I am sorry that time just slipped away so quickly. I could have done more.

Acceptance: I see my child adjusting well, finding their voice, and making the right decisions, so maybe it is OK that they are on their own. I, too, am now finding my stride and learning how to do activities that I enjoy and find fulfillment in.

Granted, you may not grieve in this manner. You may be as ready as your child is for them to assert their independence and be out on their own. For many, though, this void leaves many unresolved feelings. How do you cope with these feelings when you are roaming around in your house, and everywhere you look is a reminder of your child's absence?

Here are some coping tips I used when my children left—and in the spirit of full disclosure, many of my empty-nester friends shared these with me:

- Close the bedroom door. This was a technique I used after each of my children left for college. When the door was closed, I was able to tell myself that they were taking a nap or studying. Basically, I was psyching myself out. Confession: It works!
- Remove their chair at the dining room table or sit in their chair. Looking at my empty chair was much more comforting than looking at theirs.
- We all enjoy getting packages in the mail, and our children are no different. Send them a care package. Baking homemade cookies or sending their favorite snacks, book or memento connects you with them without physically being there. It

also lets them know you are thinking about them. After all, they are likely missing home, too.

- Send them a text every morning for the first few months to let them know you are thinking about them and want them to have a great day. I did that, hoping that if they were feeling lonely and did not want to reach out to me, they at least knew that they had an ally in their corner who was touching base with them every day.

Be Honest with Yourself

It is easy to pretend that you are doing OK to the outside world. You want others to think you are a strong person who is handling this transition with ease. And the truth is that on some days this may be true. On other days, however, you may be struggling with the loneliness, emptiness, and sadness of not having your child at home. Honestly, I bet your child is struggling with this as well.

The emotions described here are expected. This is how we handle the change with highs and lows, and everything in between. It would be best if you stayed true to who you are. Be authentic in your feelings and how they are impacting you at that moment. It is even OK for you to show your emotions to those around you in a safe environment.

Here is the scoop: Find your support group, your peer group, a confidante, your significant other, or your parents to help you get through this challenging time. Having an empty nest is not easy, and now is the time to lean on your support group to get you through.

By doing so, you will find that you are not alone. These are people who care about you, want you to be happy, and are proud that you have raised a child who is confident enough to spread their wings and begin to fly. Though these words may not be helpful initially, you will settle into this new normal in a matter of time.

Does Your Child Need You More Than You Initially Thought?

This is the real question. We have parented the best we knew how to and have given our children the tools we believe they need to achieve the success and the independence they are desiring. But what happens when they are far away and need your guidance and support?

I would guess that this happens more frequently than we can imagine.

As hard as it is on parents, it is exponentially more difficult for children. They have traded their security, family, friends, and comfort zones for a brand-new life. Many times, they are not sure that they have made the right decision. Did I choose the right college? Is this the major I want to pursue? How do I make friends (often, for the first time in their entire lives)? How do we manage our lives with no help from my parents or my support group? I have heard these questions many, many times —including when my own children called asking them.

When your children are struggling to find their new normal in their new lives, you have two options:

- You can ask them to come home if they are struggling with managing their day-to-day life. If they are not making friends, able to complete their tasks, get a good night's sleep, or are showing signs of depression or anxiety, then they may need some time at home to gather their bearings before trying again.
- If they need reassurance or answers to logistical

questions, you may be able to walk them through
their problems and provide enough verbal support
so they can gain their strength and muster through.

You will need to make a judgment call by taking cues from
what your child is sharing with you and observing their behavior. Use your parent's intuition. What is your gut feeling about
how your child is managing their new life?

Punam's Perspective

As you can likely surmise from this chapter, dropping my children off at their colleges was a harrowing event for me. I had
spent each day of their lives caring for and protecting them. It
was my job, and I took it seriously. Sometimes, a bit too seriously. Just ask any of my friends. But I wanted them to feel
secure and confident in their abilities.

So, when my husband and I took them to college, it was a
heartbreaking experience. Although they were ready to begin
their lives, a piece of mine was ending. Each time we left one of
them at college, I struggled to accept that the years with them
had flown by. Had we done enough? Had we prepared them to
be as independent as they needed to be? Were there skills they
needed that we had not taught them yet?

What I learned was that they continue to need us. Their
questions, though, now revolve around real-life challenges.
Those that will impact their futures and not always the day-to-
day challenges.

- How do I apply for a credit card?
- I need health or car insurance. Where do I go?
- How much of my earnings should I put into
  savings?

- How do I pay taxes?

By helping them with these life questions, I quickly realized that this was what we had been preparing my children for their entire lives. We raised them to be independent, free-thinking, and compassionate people. To make informed, thoughtful decisions. My husband and I had tried hard to instill these values to the best of our abilities, and when we said, "See ya later," we realized we had done just that. It was time for them to create their own paths in life.

I realized that they were OK and that it was now time to start focusing on what I wanted to be when I grew up. After many years, I was free to choose a path that was all mine. One I could create that would fulfill my passion. Having spent my entire life in education as a student, teacher, parent, volunteer, and advocate, I knew teaching would need to be a part of whatever I would pursue. After much contemplation, research, and talking to my friends and family, I decided to merge my two loves—education and speaking on my topics of interest.

I soon began this journey of helping parents become partners in their child's school to foster a successful education. It was a natural fit, as that was what I had been doing all my parenting life.

Parenting is the most rewarding job in the world. And we never know how we are doing until we see our children grow up and become independent. When they succeed and are rewarded professionally, we need to bask in the glory of a job well done.

Our time with our children is fleeting, but our impact on each other is lifelong. So, when our children head off to begin their lives, we must know that we have done our very best and be proud.

Cheers!

AFTERWORD

BY DARYL A. WARD, PH.D.

Since the main focus of this book is parent empowerment, I thought it would be fitting for you to read about the "other side" of the parent-school relationship: that of the one of the schools involved in Punam's stories. However, as I've been asked to put a "coda" on Punam's wonderful text, I want my comments to be taken in the correct light—meaning, I want to state my biases up front. Full disclosure: Punam and I are good friends and have been for many years now. With that said, my remarks that close this book are intended to be given from my perspective as a 30+ year public educator and school-based administrator—someone who worked with Punam as she put into practice (admittedly, sometimes through trial and error) the ideas and concepts you've been reading about. I hope to do this in a manner that both celebrates Punam's words and deeds, and also reveals what "parent empowerment" can mean for those choosing to embrace the notions shared in this book. As noted above, I will limit my thoughts to what this pursuit of engagement looks like in a public-school-setting; what does being a parent volunteer really mean from the perspective of the school itself?

Trust

The first element of the parent volunteer-school relationship is that of trust. Like any relationship, each person has to have a level of trust in the other for there to be any productive results from the relationship. I can't speak to how Punam developed that trust early in her parent-volunteer career, but I can say that by the time I got to know her (and her husband, Anu), her reputation preceded her: the previous schools' administrations vouched for her willingness to serve and for her ability to be trusted.

This type of trust extends beyond just "keeping a secret"—though I will add that knowing I could speak professionally, yet freely with Punam was important. When I think of the type of trust I'm really talking about here, I'm most concerned with the idea of integrity and with the concept of keeping your word. Whenever Punam said, "Anything you need, let me know and I'll be there," she meant it. I've encountered many well-meaning people who say things like that, but when you call on them for assistance, they are consistently unavailable. After a series of these encounters, you learn two things: 1) I'm not going to keep reaching out to you only to be told no and 2) you learn to recognize the rarity of those people who ARE available when they say they will be.

Punam's hallmark was her accessibility. Now, admittedly, as she'll be the first to tell you, her life situation (not having an-outside-the-home-job) offered her more flexibility in her volunteering schedule, but regardless, she made a conscious decision that because she offered her time and services, then she was going to prioritize any such requests by the school. It was not uncommon for me to call her (because, let's be honest, when I discovered she really would "drop everything and come help," then I was going to take her up on that offer!) for some assistance only to have her show up in an hour or so to get to work on the project at hand.

I could also trust Punam to give me honest answers to my questions. While I always tried to be careful about avoiding gossip (I never really found that to be professionally productive), Punam is very loyal to her relationships: to individuals and to her children's schools. Therefore, she would often give me a heads up regarding certain individuals or specific conflicts that I should be aware of. As a school principal, the one thing I hated more than anything was being surprised. I prided myself on my creative problem-solving skills and those are difficult to fully employ in an off-the-cuff manner (though I did learn to get pretty good at that too). It was helpful to have someone I trusted offering me counsel regarding unknown people and situations. Now, please note, I was always very clear with Punam (and she respected this), that I really didn't care about any petty or even severe inter-parent squabbles or jealousies; my time was too valuable to spend sorting those out. However, I was also clear that I did want to know about people or situations that would jeopardize what WAS most important to me: the health and well-being of my students, faculty, and school. Suffice it to say that not all of the constituents of a school have the best interests of the school in mind. Therefore, being able to trust Punam's thoughts regarding any possible pitfalls that I might encounter in other relationships and situations was helpful to me as a practicing administrator.

So, if you really want to know what the most important thing about parent-volunteering is to me, it's being able to be trusted. It means doing what you said you would do and honoring your commitments to the school. Unfortunately, there's no magic pill that suddenly makes you trustworthy. It comes from consistently being reliable and by not being a part of the parent-gossip machine that comes with all school settings. In short, it comes from keeping your schedule open and your mouth closed.

"Objective" Advocacy

I actually typed the subheading above with a smile; there's no such thing as objective advocacy. I have a friend and mentor who taught me early in my administrative career that you may think you have a great relationship with a person, "but if you really want to see how far that goes then mess with their kids or their paychecks." He was right. Parents are usually on your side until it's their child that needs some reprimanding or who didn't get the grade they thought they should. I don't say this to be cynical as I can also recall many instances of parental support in these situations, but it works as a general rule.

So, if you can't really be an "objective" advocate, how can you really be an effective and trustworthy (see above section) parent volunteer? By recognizing your parent-biases right up front. I am a parent myself. I certainly understand the desire and the need to support your children even when she or he makes a mistake. And there's absolutely nothing wrong with advocating on their behalf. However, if you want to be taken seriously as a parent volunteer, then you need to be realistic about how much you should advocate for your children. Let me elaborate.

My wife and I have always felt that our number one parenting job was to equip our children with the skills to be independent people. In fact, when we first became empty-nesters, people would often marvel at how well we seemed to be dealing with it. We were quick to tell them that while we missed our kids being around, we felt fulfilled in that they were doing what we'd always hoped they'd do: living their own lives in their own cities in their own ways (and, I might add, with their own money!). I've also found that most parents, when we discuss this topic, agree that they too want their children to be independent and productive citizens.

However, and here's the rub, the number one thing parents do to mess this up (despite what they say they want): IS TO DO EVERYTHING FOR THEIR CHILDREN. Nowhere is this more evident than in the school setting. From doing their child's homework (yes, this happens) to never allowing their children to struggle with anything (grades, peers, setbacks, etc.), parents are often their child's (and by consequence, their own) worst enemy in this regard. I won't belabor this point as there have been numerous books written on this subject but suffice it to say that never allowing our children to fail (or struggle) at anything is *not* preparing them for the real world of college, of work, and of life.

I've been fortunate to know all four of Punam's children— and to watch them grow into amazing young people. They all benefited from Punam's and Anu's "objective" advocacy. That is to say, their parents practiced the following model when an issue arose:

1. Have you (the children) worked out how to solve the problem on your own? Have you given any thought to the teacher's perspective? Is she/he (the teacher) correct in their response/behavior or is it a deeper concern? Have you spoken with the teacher or talked with the student you're having an issue with?

2. If necessary, they would then speak directly to the teacher/coach involved in the situation to work out

a solution. More often than not, a resolution was
found during this step.

3. If one and two above didn't provide for a solution to
the problem at hand, then they would schedule a
meeting with someone in the office—and typically
with whomever the issue had the most direct
involvement (an assistant principal or guidance
counselor). They rarely jumped straight to a
meeting with the principal.

By practicing the above model, Anu and Punam were teaching
their children that, while they cared about them and were
invested in their lives, it was *their children's* responsibility to try
and figure out how to solve their own problems. And while I
won't go to into any specific incidents that may prove embarrassing, there were several occasions in which Anu and Punam
either didn't have to get involved because their children
reached a solution on their own or they got involved in a way
that both honored their role as parents yet also honored the
professionals involved in the incident.

I must add here that I never got the impression that Punam
felt her children were never in the wrong or that they didn't
deserve the consequences of their actions. Instead, I always felt
that as long as a fair and due process had occurred, then she
and Anu would honor the resolution—even if they didn't
particularly agree with it.

As a principal, I was certainly not a fan of parent-teacher-
school conflict—what principal is? However, I also realized that
it really was a part of my job as an administrator to deal with
these issues as they occurred. Having parents who recognized
their own biases in supporting their children but who also
understood the role of the school went a long way to making
these unavoidable situations much more tenable than when

irrationality carried the day. Therefore, if you really want to be appreciated— and for that matter, taken seriously—as a valued parent volunteer, then you must work to be seen as someone who is objective when it comes to how your children behave and are treated—even when you really can't be.

Sacrificial Service

The final aspect of Punam's volunteer-character, was how she learned that sometimes the desires that she might have regarding a particular situation had to be subjected to what was in the best interest of the entire school, regardless as to how it impacted her own child. As you can imagine, this is closely related to the concept discussed in the previous section, but it's extended a bit in its scope. In a nutshell, this idea involves parents understanding that sometimes what's best for the school may not be what's best for their child. Please don't misunderstand me: I'm not referencing any kind of dire, life-altering consequence that a child has to suffer, I'm simply making the claim that really effective parent volunteers understand that instead of just volunteering at *their* child's school they are volunteering to serve *all* the children at that school.

Truth be told, most school administrators I know have a love-hate relationship with the concept of parent volunteering. We realize that we can do our jobs much more effectively and with a higher degree of impact if we have parents standing in the gap with us as we all try to make their children's school experience a better one. However, we also have to deal with too many parent volunteers who only want to do things that have a direct impact on their children without regard for how that may or may not impact the other students in the school. By "sacrific-ing" time they could be spending directly benefiting their child in an effort to support *all* children, parent volunteers can become true difference-makers.

I was fortunate to lead a school with an extremely active and engaged parent-volunteer organization. The percentage of involved parents was quite high and their support for the teachers and administration was steadfast. Punam served in numerous roles with this organization, eventually becoming the president. She, along with every other board president and board officer with whom I served, including the organization members themselves, funded extra-learning opportunities, gave of their time to serve at the school, and even attended events in which their own children weren't even participating—all because they believed that by serving everyone, the entire school was lifted up. In all my years in public education, I can honestly say the most humbled and inspired I have ever been was when I got to see how these parents consistently came together to support ALL of the students— even if the initiative in question didn't directly benefit their own child.

Putting aside our own needs and wants to meet the needs and wants of others is not an easy thing to do. However, really impactful parent volunteers—volunteers who truly are empowered—come to understand the value of this type of selflessness. Let's be honest, it's one thing to do something to take care of your own child. It's something entirely different to do something to take care of other people's children. That's what sacrificial service is all about.

Concluding Thoughts

By now, I hope you've come to realize that the overarching message of this book is one of activism—and not necessarily political or social activism (though that's also okay). By contrast, it's the idea that as parents, you don't have to sit idly by and suffer from the whims and vagaries of the tasks at hand, but instead you can actually choose to DO something. Being empowered means that, even if things are mostly out of your control, how you choose to react and respond to those situations IS within your control. Whether it's dealing with your child's school, teaching them about discrimination, or even figuring out the most productive way to schedule your day, the advice and counsel presented in this book provides the reader with ample strategies to be an "active" individual.

And if you haven't come to realize that yet—then go back and read it again.

ACKNOWLEDGMENTS

This book was just a pipe dream a few years back. Knowing that I wanted to write a book on parenting, education, and children, it took some coaxing from many of my friends to figure out exactly what I wanted to say. There are so many who have championed this cause of wanting to help parents become active in their child's schools and beyond.

I want to thank those who have helped me find my voice and given me the power to write this book.

Shannon Lanier, at a long-overdue lunch, for urging me to begin podcasting to share my parenting stories so that others may benefit. From your suggestion, this book is possible. Lenore Devore for supporting and editing the book. Your confidence and reassurance have allowed me to move this book forward to publication.

Aparna Verma for her creativity, patience, and love as she not only created the cover design for the book but also being a loving, fun confidante and partner to work with during the writing of this book. Her kindness and generosity have brought to life the vision I had for this book.

Daryl Ward, the author of this book's epilogue, entrusted me with the some of the school's more sensitive issues which not only built a true friendship, but also elevated the opportunities available to our students. Because you provided me with these opportunities in your school, I feel empowered to pursue projects such as this book once my children graduated.

Brahm Verma, my dad, for making the trek to America when you were a mere 19 year-old to pursue your professional dreams. You have always been a trailblazer and inspired me to be the same. It has been a journey of feats and challenges but you've always been steadfast in your support.

Sudha Verma, my mother, for being my strength. Watching you traverse your adopted country while maintain our culture is a remarkable accomplishment for which I am truly grateful. Your unconditional love, support, sage advice, and extreme patience have carried me throughout my life. Of all the ways I call you "Mom," "Friend" is my favorite.

My children are my purpose for striving for a better world. They are unique, inspirational, and supportive in ways I cannot fathom for their young ages. Each one of them is compassionate, thought-provoking, and kind. Regardless of their career paths, I know they will be successful because of this. It is an honor and privilege to be their mother.

Maya Saxena, my oldest daughter and guinea pig, thank you for being you. For sharing your strength, individuality, and love with me and the world. You are a true gift. Kavi Saxena, my oldest son, thank you for being the family cheerleader. Your energy and positivity are infectious, and I thank you for encouraging me along this journey. Lyla Saxena, my younger daughter, you are the epitome of tenacity. Your willingness to find a way to accomplish your goals is inspirational. India Saxena, my younger son, is the essence of thoughtfulness, kindness, and diligence. Thank you for leading by example and keeping your calm when I was not.

Anu Saxena, my husband, has stood by me, supported me, and encouraged me in all my endeavors. You have always supported my vision to help children. Your understanding of my desire to stay home with our own children so they could receive the support they needed has knowing or unknowingly, touched many other lives as well. Thank you for never saying "no" to my projects!

REFERENCES

Akpan, Nsikan. 2019. "There Is No 'Gay Gene.' There Is No 'Straight Gene.' Sexuality Is Just Complex, Study Confirms." *PBS*. NewsHour Productions. August 29. https://www.pbs.org/newshour/science/there-is-no-gay-gene-there-is-no-straight-gene-sexuality-is-just-complex-study-confirms.

Axelrod, Julie. 2016. "The Health Benefits of Journaling." *Psych Central*. Psych Central. May 17. https://psychcentral.com/lib/the-health-benefits-of-journaling#2.

Berwick, C. (2019, October 25). What Does the Research Say About Testing? Retrieved from https://www.edutopia.org/article/what-does-research-say-about-testing

Bulletin, A., & Concepcion, R. (2021, March 4). 15 Lessons the Coronavirus Pandemic Has Taught Us. Retrieved March 14, 2021, from https://www.aarp.org/health/conditions-treatments/info-2021/lessons-from-covid.html

Chakrabarty, Neelam. 2017. "Barriers to Parental Involvement in Schools and What PTAs Can Do about It." *Medium*. Medium. January 12. https://medium.com/@neelamc/

barriers-to-parental-involvement-in-schools-and-what-ptas-can-do-about-it-927fa6b2coob.

Cook, Bob. 2013. "How To Become A Better Sports Parent: Stop Caring." *Forbes*. Forbes Media. May 29. https://www.forbes.com/sites/bobcook/2013/05/29/how-to-become-a-better-sports-parent-stop-caring/.

Dunckley , Victoria L. 2017. "Why Social Media Is Not Smart for Middle School Kids." *Psychology Today*. Sussex Publishers. March 26. https://www.psychologytoday.com/us/blog/mental-wealth/201703/why-social-media-is-not-smart-middle-school-kids.

Gentry, J. R., and G. Ouellette. 2019. *Brain Words: How the Science of Reading Informs Teaching*. Stenhouse Publishers.

Gray, Max. D. 2017. "How To Cope With Empty Nest Syndrome - 9 Steps." *Onehowto.com*. Onehowto.com. January 16. https://health.onehowto.com/article/how-to-cope-with-empty-nest-syndrome-6865.html.

"Good Grades Don't Guarantee Professional Success." 2017. *Exploring Your Mind*. Exploring your mind. January 10. https://exploringyourmind.com/good-grades-dont-guarantee-professional-success/.

"How (and Why) to Start a Parent-Child Book Club." 2011. *GreatSchools.org*. GreatSchools.org. August 9. https://www.greatschools.org/gk/articles/book-clubs-for-kids/.

Hughes, Diane, and Howard Stevenson. 2016. "Talking to Kids about Discrimination." *American Psychological Association*. American Psychological Association. March 9. https://www.apa.org/topics/kids-discrimination.

Leyba, Erin. 2017. "25 Simple Self-Care Tools for Parents." *Psychology Today*. Sussex Publishers. August 18. https://www.psychologytoday.com/us/blog/joyful-parenting/201708/25-simple-self-care-tools-parents.

Nabarro, Moanikeʻala. 2020. "Experts Provide Tips for Parents during Pandemic." *University of Hawaiʻi System News*. University of Hawaiʻi . May 5. https://www.hawaii.edu/news/2020/05/05/tips-for-parents-during-pandemic/

"Parent Engagement in Schools." 2018. *Centers for Disease Control and Prevention*. Centers for Disease Control and Prevention. August 7. https://www.cdc.gov/healthyyouth/protective/parent_engagement.htm.

SANE Australia. 2018. "Exercise and Mood." *Better Health Channel*. Dept. of Health & Human Services. January. https://www.betterhealth.vic.gov.au/health/healthyliving/exercise-and-mood.

Schulte, Brigid. 2015. "Making Time for Kids? Study Says Quality Trumps Quantity." *The Washington Post*. WP Company. March 28. https://www.washingtonpost.com/local/making-time-for-kids-study-says-quality-trumps-quantity/2015/03/28/10813192-d378-11e4-8fce-3941fc548f1c_story.html.

"Screen Time and Children: How to Guide Your Child." 2019. *Mayo Clinic*. Mayo Foundation for Medical Education and Research. June 20. https://www.mayoclinic.org/healthy-lifestyle/childrens-health/in-depth/screen-time/art-20047952.

Seppälä, Emma, Christina Bradley, and Michael R. Goldstein. 2020. "Research: Why Breathing Is So Effective at Reducing Stress." *Harvard Business Review*. Harvard Business School Publishing. September 29. https://hbr.org/2020/09/research-why-breathing-is-so-effective-at-reducing-stress.

Tamer, Mary. 2014. "The Education of Immigrant Children." *Harvard Graduate School of Education*. President and Fellows of Harvard College. December 11. https://www.gse.harvard.edu/news/uk/14/12/education-immigrant-children.

ABOUT THE AUTHOR

Punam V. Saxena holds a Bachelor's degree in Psychology and a Master's in Education. Throughout her 30 years of experience between teaching and advocacy in her children's schools, she implemented several procedures that have benefited the students and administrators within the school district.

Punam is a Parent Impact Coach, speaker, podcast host of edu-Me, and now a published author. Her work focuses on bridging the gap to fostering a stronger relationship between parents and schools by empowering parents to become partners in their child's education.

She has been recognized as Volunteer of the Year at Harrison School for the Arts and has received a Key to the City both in Lakeland, Florida. She has been featured in the magazines *Podcast Movement* and *Shoutout Atlanta* and spoken at several mainstage events including the Passionistas Project's *I'm Speaking*, Podcast Movement's Virtual Summit, and International Parenting Summit.

She enjoys running, cooking, reading, and spending time with her family.

- facebook.com/theedume
- twitter.com/edume19
- instagram.com/theedume
- linkedin.com/in/punam-saxena-m-ed-7981b9124